himalayan
buddhist monasteries

M.N. RAJESH
THOMAS L. KELLY

Lustre Press
Roli Books

ISBN: 81-7436-054-9

First published in 1998 as
The Buddhist Monastery by Lustre Press
© Roli & Janssen BV 2005
This revised edition published in India
by Roli Books in arrangement with
Roli & Janssen BV, The Netherlands
M-75, Greater Kailash-II Market
New Delhi 110 048, India.
Phone: ++91-11-29212271, 29212782
Fax: ++91-11-29217185
Email: roli@vsnl.com; Website: rolibooks.com

Editor: Nandita Jaishankar
Design: Inkspot
Layout: Naresh Mondal

Printed and bound in Singapore

♣ **PRECEDING PAGE 1:** A GENEN, OR ABBOT MONK
AT LINGSHED MONASTERY IN LADAKH, INDIA.

♣ **PRECEDING PAGES 2-3:** SWAYAMBHUNATH
STUPA, KATHMANDU, NEPAL.

♣ STACKED LIKE MATCHBOXES, KI MONASTERY,
SPITI, INDIA, USES EVERY INCH OF SPACE AVAILABLE
IN THE HILLY TERRAIN. THE BASEMENT HAS A CACHE
OF ARMS, THE REMAINS OF A TURBULENT PAST.

contents

Introduction

Little is known about the monasteries that dot the region of the Himalayas. Spreading from Ladakh, Lahaul, Spiti and Kinnaur to Sikkim and Bhutan, a mystic value is attached to these places even today. Over the centuries, these monasteries have been depicted as places far removed in time and space, places where time stands still like the barren landscape and the surrounding rarefied air, devoid of the chirping of birds. Though many centuries have passed by, several things still remain the same—the age-old monastic ceremonies, the warmth of the people and their religious fervour manifested in numerous festivals. Like the travellers of the 19th century, explorers, linguists, scholars, botanists and adventurers even today can see, all along the Himalayas, people listening with rapt attention to tales indicating the charm of the region. It is very difficult to describe in a few words what accounts for the mystique of the monasteries in this region which is a cultural zone and an extension of the Tibetan cultural area extending from Ladakh in the west to Sikkim, parts of Nepal and Tawang in the east, to as far as the frontiers of China, Mongolia and Russia respectively. Time-honoured rituals and social conventions established under the influence of the Vajrayana school of Buddhism flourishes here, overseeing the continuity of traditions. Generations of people come and go, centring their lives around the monasteries, locally called gompas. Perched on hilltops, cliffs and overlooking precipices, they seem to be floating clouds in a realm entirely their own. Being the repositories of Tibetan culture, the gompas embody a living tradition. Monks clad in red can be seen going about with their prayer wheels, dutifully praying for society.

With prayer flags fluttering in the background, the gompa breaks the silence of the rugged landscape with its sacred ritual dances, chants, music and chiming bells. Words cannot fully capture the magic of the Himalayan monasteries. Their mystic calm, even today, lends to the amazing tales of travellers that can be heard in all the small town cafes dotting the last outposts to the inaccessible valleys that open out a gateway to another century—the gompa.

♣ FACING PAGE: MONKS DANCING ROUND THE FLAGPOLE IN MATHO MONASTERY IN LADAKH, INDIA. THE DANCE ENDS WITH THE DISMEMBERING OF AN EFFIGY MADE OF FLOUR, SYMBOLIZING THE DESTRUCTION OF EVIL.

♣ A SIMPLE BOOM LAMA (OR TANTRIC ADEPT) OF THE TIBETAN BUDDHIST LAMA NYINGMA SECT, LIVES WITH HIS CHILDREN AND FAMILY AT THE DHIGA VILLAGE CAVE RETREAT IN THE HUMLA REGION OF NEPAL.

♣ FOLLOWING PAGES 10-11: THE MAJESTIC TABO MONASTERY IN SPITI, INDIA. FOUNDED IN 996 AD, TABO IS THE BIGGEST AND THE OLDEST SURVIVING MONASTERY IN INDIA. IT CELEBRATED ITS 1000TH ANNIVERSARY IN 1996 WHEN HIS HOLINESS THE DALAI LAMA INITIATED THE KALACHAKRA CEREMONY.

♣ IN HUMLA, NEPAL, THE PRACTICE OF POLYANDRY IS STILL COMMON AMONG NOMADS. SEEN HERE ARE FIVE BROTHERS AT THEIR POLYANDROUS MARRIAGE CEREMONY. IT IS BELIEVED THAT POLYANDRY KEEPS BROTHERS TOGETHER AND MAKES FOR A STRONG AND STABLE HOUSEHOLD. THE POPULATION IS LESS AND WEALTH IS CONCENTRATED WITH BROTHERS WORKING TOGETHER.

three
jewels

Prince Siddhartha Gautama, later known as the Buddha or the Enlightened One, was the founder of the Buddhist Holy Order, or Sangha. He was born a prince in the 6th century BC in the sacred grove of sal trees in Lumbini on a full moon night. His father Suddhodana, the chief of the Sakya clan, summoned the royal astrologer. After much goading from the king, Prince Siddhartha's prophecy was spelt out. According to the signs and the time of his birth, the royal astrologer prophesized that the prince would either renounce the world or become a world conqueror. Lest the first part of the prophecy come true, Siddhartha was brought up in extraordinary comfort and shielded from the outside world by his father. The young prince cultivated all the arts and statecraft expected of a nobleman. He married at the right age and sired a son named Rahula.

One day, while the prince was on his daily sojourn, the royal charioteer Channana accompanied him and also answered his queries. But the sequence of events did not materialize as his father would have wanted them to. After seeing four sights over a period of time—a sick man, an old man, a corpse and a monk (an oft repeated theme in Buddhist art)—a fundamental transformation crept into the prince. Prince Siddhartha was very moved; he became restless and sorrowful. When he asked Channana about the last sight, the charioteer explained to him that this was a monk, a person who had renounced the bonds binding him to the material world. Now Prince Siddhartha saw a means to eliminating sorrow and began to see material life as futile and full of grief. One full-moon night in the month of Asada,

♣ FACING PAGE: DETAIL OF A GUILDED IMAGE OF MAITREYA, THE FUTURE BUDDHA, AT THIKSE MONASTERY IN LADAKH, INDIA. INFLUENCED BY CHINESE ART, THE BUDDHA HERE IS DISTINCTIVELY MONGOLOID, SEEN IN THE TREATMENT OF THE NOSE, CHEEKBONES AND THE EYES.

There are many paintings and sculptures of this stage of the Buddha's life, where he was labelled the emaciated Buddha, to drive home the point that forceful asceticism is not productive—on the contrary, it is harmful to the body.

Siddhartha finally set out on the right path and sat down to meditate. After severe meditation for forty-nine days under the bodhi (*Ficus religiosa*) tree, a demon (which, according to Buddhist cosmology, is actually a creation of the mind), called Mara tried to tempt Siddhartha with images of luxury and ravishing damsels. But Siddhartha was engrossed in meditation; he conquered all these influences and in the end emerged supreme by finally conquering desire. Mara asked for proof of enlightenment and Siddhartha pointed his index finger towards the ground calling upon Bhoomidevi or Mother Earth as witness to his enlightenment. Siddhartha attained enlightenment and henceforth became known as the Buddha or the Enlightened One. Bhumisparsa (calling the Earth to witness enlightenment) mudra is one of the six important mudras (mudras being a symbolic language used as a means of non-verbal communication in performing arts and aesthetics). Even today, the devout can see the same tree at Bodhgaya where the Buddha attained enlightenment. Incidentally, this is a sapling of the earlier tree that was taken to Sri Lanka in the ancient period. Bodhgaya is the holiest place for Buddhists—according to Buddhist sacred geography, it is at the centre of the universe.

The Buddha then began to preach the theory of the Middle Path that lies between the extremes of asceticism and hedonism. This is called the Dhammacahhapavattana, or the Turning of the Wheel of Law, meaning the exposition of the Four

♣ A TRADITIONAL THANGKA (A TIBETAN RELIGIOUS SCROLL OR HOLY PAINTING) AT THIKSE MONASTERY, LADAKH, INDIA.

Noble Truths and the Eight Fold Path, which are the cardinal principles of Buddhism. The core of the Buddha's teachings is based on the simple premise that all existence is painful. Human beings do not realise that it is those conditions which they are accustomed to that give rise to sorrow. In other words, all existence is tied to the notion that a person has desires. From these desires flow more desires —desire is the root cause of all destruction. Since there is a craving to fulfill desire, it is this craving that leads to more and more bondage and unhappiness. Thus arises a contradiction: all that a person desires is impermanent like the person himself and this leads him to be caught up in the endless cycle of birth and rebirth as there is no end to desire. All understanding is clouded by ignorance, which acts as smoke, screening the perception of reality. The implicit awareness that the world is transitory is the starting point. The Buddha then shows a clear path to come out of this morass. They are the Four Noble Truths or the Cattari Ariya Saccani:

The world is full of suffering and misery.
Desire is the main cause of suffering.
The path to end suffering is to end desire.
There is a path to end desire.

The path to end desire is called the Eight Fold Path or the Ashtangika Marga, which stresses on the eight conditions, namely: right views, right aspirations, right speech, right conduct, right livelihood, right effort, right mindfulness, and right meditational attainment. The term 'right' (true or correct) is used to distinguish sharply between the precepts of the Buddha and other teachings.

Soon, the new religion gained its first adherents in Benares, Rajagriha and Uruvavilva, both among the common people and nobility and royalty. The followers of the new religion were called bhikkus (those who had renounced the world). There were also other lay followers who believed in the philosophy but led a householder's life and were called upasakas, or upasikas, if female.

The Buddha, the Dharma (Faith) and the Sangha (Order) are the three jewels or triratna of Buddhism and whenever anyone becomes a convert, he utters these words, 'I take refuge in the Buddha, I take refuge in the Dharma, I take refuge in the Sangha.' The four assemblies of the Buddhist Sangha are composed of bhikkus (monks), bhikkunis (nuns), upasakas (laymen) and upasikas (laywomen). Initially women were forbidden in the Sangha. It was five years after the Buddha's enlightenment that a delegation of five hundred Sakyan women, led

♣ SERA MONASTERY, TIBET. SERA, GADAN AND DREPUNG MONASTERIES ARE KNOWN AS THE THREE GREAT MONASTERIES OF TIBET. CONTRARY TO COMMON BELIEF, THESE MONASTERIES ARE NOT PLACES OF WORSHIP BUT ARE MONASTIC UNIVERSITIES PROVIDING RELIGIOUS EDUCATION TO THE MONKS.

by his aunt Prajapathi Gautami, went to the Buddha requesting permission to become nuns. The Buddha initially refused. It is said that Prajapathi Gautami and the five hundred women shaved their heads and donned the orange robes of the Order and again appeared before the Buddha, who then relented and acceded to their request.

The Buddha lived till the age of 80 and is said to have travelled with his followers all over the vast Gangetic plains preaching the doctrine in a simple form that struck a receptive chord among the masses. One of the devices he used was to preach in the form of examples; even today, the Dhammapada (literally, in the steps of the Dhamma) a collection of sayings on many topics attributed to the Buddha clearly brings out the effective method of

♣ IN KUSHINAGAR, INDIA, A PILGRIM MEDITATES IN FRONT OF AN IMAGE OF THE BUDDHA IN HIS FINAL SAMADHI, A LIBERATED STATE BEYOND DEATH OR REBIRTH.

transmission as the following description shows:

> The fool who knows that he is a fool is a wiser man than the wise man who does not know he is a fool.

The Buddhist community started to grow and there was a need for the proper organization of the monastic order. Hence a set of rules, the Vinaya Pitaka, was drawn up. Vinaya means rules and Pitaka means basket, since early Buddhist literature was divided into three baskets: the Vinaya Pitaka or the canonical law (followed even today in all Buddhist monasteries), the Sutta Pitaka or the sayings of the Buddha and the Abhidamma Pitaka dealing with metaphysics. In the Vinaya Pitaka we find the rules that the monks and nuns are supposed to follow,

expounded by Upali, one of the Buddha's earliest disciples. Upali was said to have attended the first Buddhist Council held after the mahaparinirvana (the final liberation from death and rebirth) of the Buddha. The rules contained in the Vinaya Pitaka are hence attributed to the sayings of the Buddha himself and were arrived at after a great deal of thought and pragmatism. The rules are not stringent and it is enough that the laity follows the five great abstentions: not taking life, not drinking intoxicants, not stealing, not telling a lie and not leading an unchaste life. But the monks have to follow a harder set of rules, the four rules of monastic austerity and the four great prohibitions: sexual intercourse, theft,

murder and false or self-interested usurpation, the violation of any of which leads to automatic expulsion from the monastery. The rules for the nuns were closely modelled on those for monks. Today the total number of rules in the monasteries is 227, 225 and 250 in the Pali, Chinese and Tibetan Buddhist canons respectively. It also should be noted that all the rules are not the same in the three traditions of Buddhism, as they evolved under different historical conditions over twenty-five centuries. The Vinaya Pitaka also contained rules for admission to the Order, for regular assembly, collection of alms, and retreat to approved places of residence during the rainy season and for everyday life. There were

♣ A SPLENDID 15 METRE TALL GUILDED IMAGE OF MAITREYA, OR FUTURE BUDDHA, DOMINATES THE ENTRANCE (SPLIT INTO TWO LEVELS) IN THIKSE MONASTERY, LADAKH, INDIA. THE MAITREYA BUDDHA TEMPLE IS ESPECIALLY NOTEWORTHY AS IT WAS RECENTLY RESTORED.

general instructions against idle gossip, evil friends and pleasure seeking. The monks were advised to be self-possessed and composed; this high standard of morality was supposed to serve as an exemplary model.

In the early Buddhist Sangha, the monks had very few personal possessions, just enough to lead a frugal life. These included the three robes consisting of an outer garment, an undergarment and a cloak (nuns were permitted a belt and a shirt), all in yellow or red to indicate renunciation. The Tibetan monks and nuns wear maroon coloured robes. Other possessions included a begging bowl, a razor for shaving, a needle, a strainer, a staff and a toothpick. For monks from cold countries, the use of shoes was permitted along with caps. In Mahayana Buddhism (the Greater Vehicle, the branch of Buddhism which aims at universal salvation) monks can also have the rosary, as it is an integral part of their meditation.

Monks could be drawn from all castes. This served as a great liberating route to many people who were stigmatised on account of their low birth in early Indian society. Till today, many people born in lower castes in the Hindu system, convert to Buddhism.

However, people accused of crime, slaves, debtors and those suffering from contagious diseases are not allowed. This is because they do not come with strong religious convictions but view monkhood only as a means to end their misery.

The ideal of the monk is the propagation of the Dharma among the laity and the attainment of enlightenment. He is supposed to rise early in the day, meditate, then dress and go out to the nearest settlement in search of alms, return to the monastery and give spiritual instruction to the laity. As monks are not allowed to take part in any commercial activity, they are totally dependent on the lay community for food and sustenance.

The spread of Buddhism led to many merchants and rulers patronising the new religion. The kshatriyas or the warriors, who were the hereditary rulers, supported Buddhism to counteract the influence of the brahmanas (the priestly class). One of the greatest rulers to patronise Buddhism was the Emperor Ashoka, who is said to have built

84,000 stupas (a mound-like structure known as chorten in Tibetan, which means a reliquary object). This may not fit in with the exact historical records but the number 84,000 is a conventional number in India like 1,008, 101, and so on, and therefore has to be seen in that light. Today we find the Buddhist wheel of Emperor Ashoka adopted as the state emblem of India.

Merchants were economically well placed in Indian society during the period of the Buddha since the prevalence of a money economy, guilds and general prosperity emerged at this time. In spite of being prosperous, the merchants were placed below the brahmanas and the kshatriyas, in terms of ritual ranking. This could not be changed since one could not change one's birth. Therefore, Buddhism was a pragmatic alternative, as it did not recognize any differences based on one's birth but only on one's karma. New adherents brought in more donations, particularly the mercantile classes. They also patronized Buddhism, as the principle of non-

♣ LEFT: YOUNG MONKS READ SCRIPTURES AT A MONASTERY IN MOUNT KAILASH, TIBET.

♣ RIGHT: YAKPA MONASTERY, A NYINGMA SECT NUNNERY IN HUMLA REGION, NEPAL. A NUN RECITES PRAYERS AT A DEUKI (OR DEWAKI) CEREMONY, WHERE A YOUNG GIRL IS OFFERED AT THE ALTAR OF THE DEITIES IN EXCHANGE FOR BETTER FORTUNE.

violence was conducive to trade. Therefore it is not surprising that a very large number of the early monasteries like the famed Sanchi stupa were situated on the main trade routes. The monasteries also served as places where caravans could rest during their long sojourn and be assured that they would not be attacked, since robbers spared the monasteries on account of their sacred nature. The monks were well versed in medicine and treated the traders during their stay at the monasteries and thus traders donated generously to monasteries.

As the monks did not have any permanent residence, they lived a nomadic life, staying under trees and in caves. During the course of their wanderings, the monks would engage in debates. During the rainy season the issue of travel came up. However much they tried to avoid it, the monks often trampled upon the lush green vegetation that was spread all around. This posed a dilemma, as travel would take the life of the newly sprouted plants. Thus the Buddha asked the monks to remain at one place and travel was prohibited during the rainy season. During this period, they were required to live within a prescribed boundary, called the vassavasa. Subsequently, resting places called aramas came up to serve the monks during the rainy season, which became a period of retreat and introspection. In the course of time, these places came to be known as viharas or residences where the wandering monks formed the Sanghas. Donations led to

♣ THE VENERABLE CHOKYI NYIMA RINPOCHE. AS THE OLDEST SON OF URGYEN TULKU RINPOCHE, HE WAS RECOGNIZED AT 18 MONTHS OF AGE AS THE SEVENTH INCARNATION OF GAR DRUBCHEN, A DRIKUNG KAGYU MASTER AND EMANATION OF NAGARJUNA, BY THE 16TH GYALWANG KARMAPA. SOON AFTER HE WAS ENTHRONED AT HIS PREDECESSOR'S MONASTERY, DRONG GON TUBTEN DARGYE LING MONASTERY, IN NAKCHUKHA, CENTRAL TIBET.

the expansion of the viharas and they proliferated all over eastern India. Interestingly, the modern Indian state of Bihar gets its name from vihara since this was the land of the Buddha's birth and was studded with innumerable viharas. As Buddhism spread among the laity and monasteries became permanent institutions, the laity supported the upkeep of the monks which was seen as a meritorious act leading to the accumulation of good karma, the monks and nuns had a lot of time at their disposal. Therefore we see a creative abundance of literature, philosophy and also other works such as medicinal texts and works on grammatology authored by

monks. The nuns were also not far behind — the popular *Therigatha* was composed during the early period of Buddhism. Thus the developments in Buddhist philosophy also made the monks more sedentary and the viharas became permanent residences. This was the picture of Buddhism during its early days.

Questions of philosophy and monastic discipline constituted points of discord, often leading to the emergence of new sects. According to the Chinese traveller Huien Tsang, there were as many as eighteen sects of Buddhism in India which he visited in the 7th century.

♣ YOUNG MONKS SIT ALIGNED AND RECITE PRAYERS AT THE CREMATION CEREMONY OF URGYEN TULKU RINPOCHE IN PUCHANG, NEPAL.

♣ FACING PAGE: INSIDE THE NECHUNG MONASTERY, TIBET, SEAT OF THE STATE ORACLE, PILGRIMS COME TO WORSHIP THE PROTECTOR DEITY, PEHAR.

♣ THE TULKU OF TASHILUNPO MONASTERY, SHIGASTE, TIBET, LEADING A PRAYER SESSION. ALONG WITH INDIVIDUAL SALVATION, BUDDHIST MONKS ALSO PRAY FOR THE WELL-BEING OF ENTIRE MANKIND.

from vihara to
mahavihara

Viharas or monasteries were now transformed to mahaviharas. The word 'maha' is used as a prefix in India to indicate grandeur like the Mahabharata or the great epic, but in the case of the mahavihara we would be at fault to translate the same as a great vihara since there were many qualitative changes. The first of these was the focus on education and advanced learning. Thus mahaviharas are properly known as monastic universities or doctrinal colleges. We see a proliferation of great mahaviharas from as far as Taxila and Orgyan in the extreme northwest to Kashmir in the north and as far as Magadha and Bengal in the east which were the heartland of Buddhism. The great monastic universities of Nalanda, Vikramashila and Odantapuri evolved into centres of advanced learning where new ideas in philosophy emerged constantly enriched by scholars and students from many parts of Asia like Burma, Malaya, Java, Sumatra, Nepal, Sri Lanka Tibet, China and other regions. These monastic universities represent a stage in the evolution of Buddhism over a long period and formed the model for the establishment of similar large-scale monastic universities in different parts of Asia, particularly the Tibetan cultural area.

Around 800 AD, the Mahayana school began to outnumber other sects of Buddhism in India. The basic difference among the earlier schools and Mahayana is the concept of the Bodhisattva. The achievement of nirvana or salvation is not confined to an initiated monk and the Bodhisattva is one who holds back his own

♣ **FACING PAGE:** PARO MONASTERY IN BHUTAN IS KNOWN AS RINCHEN PUNG DZONG, OR 'FORTRESS ON A HEAP OF JEWELS.' BUILT IN 1646, THE FORTRESS WAS USED ON NUMEROUS OCCASIONS TO DEFEND THE PARO VALLEY FROM INVASIONS BY TIBET. THE MONASTERY WAS FORMERLY THE MEETING HALL FOR THE NATIONAL ASSEMBLY AND NOW HOUSES THE PARO MONASTIC SCHOOL AND GOVERNMENT OFFICES.

salvation to help others attain theirs. The earlier Theravada school (the Lesser Vehicle, or the branch of Buddhism which aims at individual salvation) gave way to the Mahayana concept of the 'saviour.' Here we see that the emphasis is not on individual salvation, but the concern for all sentient beings and a societal base that is at the heart of the Bodhisattva ideal. It closely fitted in with the concept of a saviour, an image that was very popular among the different brahmanical sects in contemporary India.

Developing from the Mahayana was the Vajrayana (literally, thunderbolt) form of Buddhism, also referred to as Tantric Buddhism. Here the view is one in which enlightenment arises from the realization that opposing principles are in truth really one. It is this form of Buddhism that is followed in what is known as the Tibetan cultural area, or the Lamaist Himalayas. It would be appropriate to use the term Tibetan cultural area to refer to the vast areas comprising Tibet, Ladakh, Lahaul, Spiti, Kinnaur (all in the western Himalayas in India), the Indian state of Sikkim, and the adjacent kingdom of Bhutan. The northern areas of Nepal where the Sherpas live and the areas of Manang, Lo, Mustang and Dolpo are the Tibetan cultural areas in Nepal. In the extreme northwestern flank of India, in the state of Arunachal Pradesh, lies the Tawang corridor adjacent to Tibet which is also part of the Tibetan cultural area. Beyond Tibet lie Mongolia and the Mongol territories of Buryatiya and Kalmykia, which are autonomous republics within the Russian federation and are also part of the Tibetan cultural area. It is interesting to note that Kalmykia is the only Buddhist political entity in Europe. The Tibetan cultural area is referred to on the basis that,

♣ EARLY MORNING FOG SHROUDS THE FINAL RESTING PLACE OF THE BUDDHA WHERE HE ATTAINED SAMADHI, A LIBERATED STATE BEYOND DEATH OR REBIRTH. KUSHINAGAR, INDIA.

♣ FOLLOWING PAGES 36-37: STATUES OF THE BUDDHA IN VARIOUS POSES AT THIKSE MONASTERY IN LADAKH, INDIA. EACH GESTURE SIGNIFIES AN ABSTRACT PRINCIPLE; THE HAIR IS DONE IN DISTINCTIVE GANDHARA (INDO-GREEK) STYLE.

even though all of the people there do not speak Tibetan, the greater tradition in all these areas is Tibetan and they all follow Tibetan Buddhism. Thus we see the use of Tibetan in ritual and religious traditions of all these areas, where the monastic customs are the same. It is for this reason that Tibetan is sometimes referred to as the Latin of Central Asia.

The Tibetan cultural area is historically important in the reconstruction of Buddhist history since we see here the great monasteries continuing traditions from many hundreds of years. One of the oft quoted and classic examples would be that of Tabo, the oldest continuously functioning monastery in India founded in 996 AD. To understand the Tibetan Buddhist monastery, we have to first

get a glimpse of the history of the Tibetan cultural areas that would help us place in a better perspective the role of monasteries. To begin with, we see that the Tibetan plateau is a very harsh environment characterized by vast stretches of wasteland and valley amidst mountain ranges all situated on an average elevation of about 15,000 feet. In this harsh terrain dwelt many Tibetan tribes who cultivated barley and herded yaks for a living. During the 7th century AD, the emergence of a very strong king in Tibet called Songtsen Gampo united the various tribes on the Roof of the World and built a formidable empire. Not resting with building an empire, the great king is also credited with some major cultural achievements, like the introduction of Buddhism into Tibet and a script for the

Tibetan language, both of which came from India. The strong emperor of Tibet extended his arms as far as Nepal and China and forced the rulers there to give their daughters in marriage to him and subsequently married Brihukuti Devi, the daughter of King Anshuvarman of Nepal and Princess Wen Chen Kong Jo, a Chinese princess. Both the queens are now worshipped in Tibet as the Green Tara and the White Tara respectively. It was at this time that the emperor sent a group of seven Tibetans to India to see whether Tibetans could become monks. After they returned, Buddhism was inaugurated in Tibet.

It was during this period (9-11th centuries AD) that all the Tibetan cultural areas saw the spread of Buddhist influence. In Tibetan Buddhism, we see the presence of four main sects called the Nyingma, Kagyu, Sakya and the Geluk, each with a number of sub-sects. The reason for the widespread acceptance of Buddhism lies in the fact that the Mahayana school has incorporated elements from Bon, the pre-Buddhist religion of this area. The founder of the Bon religion was Lord Sherab Miwo who is said to have systematized earlier animistic beliefs. Though they are not Buddhists, Bonpos also have monasteries and follow practices similar to that of the Buddhists, and can be found all over the Himalayan region. It would be out of place to use the word sect here, though it is used in all the European texts on Buddhism. The Buddhists themselves prefer the word movement since the word sect is indicative of separatist tendencies.

♣ AT TASHI-TOH IN NORTHERN TIBET, THE ROCK FORMATIONS HAVE RICH MYTHOLOGICAL AND MYSTICAL ASSOCIATIONS FOR BUDDHISTS.

♣ PEMA WONGCHEN, THE REINCARNATION OF A LAMA, WITH HIS FATHER RALO RINPOCHE AND HIS MOTHER. IN IDENTIFYING A REINCARNATION OF A LAMA, THE CHILD IS BROUGHT TO THE MONASTERY BY HIS PARENTS AND SUBJECTED TO A TEST WHEREIN ARTICLES OF THE DECEASED LAMA LIKE PRAYER WHEELS AND ROSARIES, ALONG WITH MANY DUPLICATES ARE PLACED BEFORE THE CHILD. THE BLESSED CHILD SELECTS THE ITEMS WHICH WERE THE PERSONAL POSSESSIONS OF THE LAMA.

The Nyingma is the oldest Buddhist sect that was founded under the patronage of King Trisong Detsen, the second great emperor of Tibet after Songtsen Gampo. During his reign Santirakshata, the abbot of the Nalanda monastery was invited to build a monastery in Tibet called the Samye monastery. When the learned Santirakshata commenced the work, he saw that whatever work was done in the day was being undone at night and therefore he suggested to the Emperor to invite Acharya Padmasambhava, the abbot of the Vikramashila monastery who was very powerful in Tantric lore. Guru Padmasambhava, the 8th-century Indian Buddhist saint who visited Tibet and who is sometimes called the second Buddha, tamed the spirits that were causing the destruction and appropriated them as the tutelary deities in the Tibetan pantheon. He is well remembered for his role in the propagation of Buddhism in Tibet and the sect founded by him is called the Nyingma. Nyingma monks do not strictly adhere to celibacy and till recently they followed the strange custom of sticking out their tongue while greeting fellow monks. This practice began under the reign of the apostate King Lang Darma who terrorized and

♣ TASHILUNPO MONASTERY IN TIBET IS THE SEAT OF THE PANCHEN LAMAS, TUTORS OF THE DALAI LAMAS. FOUNDED IN 1447 AD, IT IS VIRTUALLY A MONASTIC TOWN WITH MORE THAN TWO THOUSAND RESIDENT MONKS AND SEVERAL BUDDHIST COLLEGES.

♣ A MONK OFFERS
PRAYERS TO THE
MAIN IDOL OF THE
SEATED BUDDHA
KEPT INSIDE
TASHILUNPO
MONASTERY,
SHIGATSE, TIBET.
THE SEATED
POSTURE IS CALLED
ASANA AND THE
HAND IS HELD UP
IN A PROTECTIVE
GESTURE.

persecuted Buddhists. In the persecution campaigns against Buddhism between the 9th and 11th centuries, Nyingmas were singled out and identified by their tongues: the constant chanting of mantras had apparently blackened them, thus giving them away.

The Kagyu sect was founded by the great Siddha (Perfected One) Tilopa. Siddha Tilopa master to the disciple. Milarepa is also revered as the greatest poet of Tibet. The Kagyus, like the Nyingmas, allow their monks to marry.

The Sakya sect is the first among the reformed sects and was founded during the second diffusion of Buddhism in the 11th century. Buddhism entered Tibet in the 8th century—after an initial tussle with the Bon

♣ A VIEW OF THE POTALA PALACE FROM THE JHOKHANG TEMPLE, LHASA, TIBET. THE POTALA PALACE, WINTER PALACE OF THE DALAI LAMA SINCE THE 7TH CENTURY, SYMBOLIZES TIBETAN BUDDHISM AND ITS CENTRAL ROLE IN THE TRADITIONAL ADMINISTRATION OF TIBET.

mastered Tantra (an ancient Hindu system of ritualistic meditation, symbolizing the basic duality of manifestation, represented by a male deity locked in sexual embrace with a female partner) from the great Indian masters. Naropa, Marpa and Milarepa are some of the great adepts of this sect. The Kagyus lay stress on practical mysticism and the direct transmission of esoteric teaching from the religion, it was firmly established. This is known as the first diffusion of Buddhism. It suffered persecution during the reign of Lang Darma when it was wiped out from central Tibet. Under the patronage of Ye-She-O, Buddhist revival started from western Tibet. This is called the second diffusion of Buddhism, during which period most gompas of the Lamaist Himalayas, like Tabo,

♣ RETREAT CAVES
IN LUBRAK, NEPAL.
MONKS USUALLY
WITHDRAW INTO
COMPLETE
DARKNESS TO
MEDITATE FOR
AS LONG AS
THREE YEARS. BY
EXTINGUISHING
LIGHT IN THEIR
LIVES, THEY HOPE
TO ULTIMATELY FIND
THE LUMINOUS
LIGHT RESIDING
WITHIN
THEMSELVES.

were founded. According to Buddhist chronicles, Rinchenzangpo built a total of 108 monasteries under the patronage of Ye-She-O. Some of the monasteries of this period have survived like the famous Alchi, which is called the Ajanta of the Himalayas on account of the large number of paintings found here in the Ajanta style.

Konchogyal Pho (1034-1102 AD) systematized the teachings of his teacher Padmasambhava, which form the basic tenets of the Sakya sect. The tenets insist on the primacy of the original Buddhist scriptures over later Tantric rituals, with particular stress on celibacy and monastic discipline. The Lamdre is the distinct teaching of the Sakyapas integrating Tantra and the Sutra (the Buddhist canon). Abbotship among the Sakyapas is hereditary passing from uncle to nephew. The most famous Sakyapa was Sakya Pandita (1182-1291 AD). There was great political turmoil in the whole of central Asia during the 13th century and later, owing to the depredations of the Mongols. Tibet was about to be annexed by the Mongols, who sent their emissaries asking for the Sakyapas to surrender. None would refuse to surrender to the might of the Mongols whose legendary armies had wrought havoc on region after region. At this time the chief abbot of the Sakyapas, the learned Sakya Pandita, went along with his nephews Phagspa and Pahgne Dorje to the Mongol camp—what followed later is history. The Mongols were so impressed by the erudition of the monks that not only did they spare Tibet but also converted to Buddhism and thus

♣ TOLING, WESTERN TIBET IS A PART OF ZHANGZHUNG, A PRE-BUDDHIST CIVILIZATION IN THE DESERT REGION SURROUNDING MOUNT KAILASH.

began a new chapter in the history of Buddhism. Mongol patronage and the establishment of Mongolian lordship over China under Kublai Khan saw many new monasteries being built all over Tibet and older monasteries being expanded. From the 13th century onwards we see that the Mongols have become Tibetanized and adopted Tibetan Buddhism as their religion.

Monasteries became powerful and sprung up all over Tibet. A large population entered the order as lamas (monks) or anis (nuns) and according to estimates, the figures ranged from nineteen per cent as suggested by some historians, and as high as twenty-five per cent, as opined by Tibetan historians. Political power shifted to the monasteries as they became the dominant factor in Tibetan life,

slowly eclipsing the role of kings. Finally, the Mongols killed the last ruler, the king of Tsang in the 14th century and Tibet was ruled by monasteries. Due to wars and clashes between the different sects, the original message of Buddhism was lost and the mass of the people faced a dilemma.

It was around this time, in a period of general crisis, the rise of the Gelukpa sect (also called the Yellow Hats) was founded by Tsong-kha-pha (1357-1419 AD) to drive home the message of the Buddha which was being obscured by other reasons. To motivate the people, the great Tsong-kha-pha gave a famous quotation: 'The toughest path to find is the most unprecedented path,' and based on this premise he founded a new sect called the Geluk. The basic principles of this sect are celibacy and the maintenance of moral standards. One of the main strengths of the Gelukpas was to counter the general impression among the public that the monks had become more interested in the material world; hence their insistence on the high moral standards of the monks to give them a moral leadership. They lay great stress on monastic discipline and an intensive study of the Mahayana Sutras according to the *Lam Rim*, the principal doctrinal book of the Gelukpas. Another innovation of the new sect was the concept of reincarnation that was borrowed from the Indian theory of avatars. According to these principles, many great lamas are reborn in another body. The Dalai Lama is the head of the Gelukpa sect and the spiritual and temporal leader of Tibet. Etymologically, the words 'Dalai Lama' mean Ocean of Wisdom and are of Mongolian origin bestowed by the Mongol patrons. In the person of the Dalai Lama, we see the reincarnation of Avalokiteswara, the Bodhisattva of Compassion, known in Tibetan as Chenrezi. Dalai Lamas can be born in any place in the Tibetan cultural area—the fourth Dalai Lama was a Mongolian prince, while the sixth Dalai Lama was from Tawang, which is in modern day India. After the death of the Dalai Lama or any reincarnate Lama, there is a search for the soul of the Lama on the basis of certain auspicious signs. Three identical sets of articles used by the deceased Lamas are kept and the person successful in identifying the right set of articles is then chosen.

♣ THE REMAINS OF INCREDIBLE STRUCTURES HANGING ON CLIFFS DESTROYED BY THE CHINESE IN 1959 IN PHUNTSOLING, TIBET.

♣ A LAMA ERECTS A
LUNGTA, BUDDHIST
PRAYER FLAG, IN
THE HIGHLAND
SUMMER PASTURES.
LUNGTA, WHICH
MEANS
'WINDHORSE,' IS
SAID TO BROADCAST
THE WORD OF THE
DHARMA (BUDDHIST
DOCTRINE) TO ALL
WHO PASS BY.

gompa community
and patronage

The most powerful and stable institution in Lamaist Himalaya is the gompa. Gompa is the literal translation of the word 'vihara' and all over the Lamaist Himalayas, including Tibet, the total number of gompas is estimated to be around 4,400. In addition we also have many old gompas that have fallen into disuse but are still preserved in a good shape on account of the aridity. Except in parts of Mongolia where we find mobile monasteries made of tents, all other gompas are proper structures. Few religious institutions in any society can claim to have such a far-reaching influence on the lives of each of its members.

The tradition started with the Buddha himself who commanded the monks to go forth in all directions and work for the betterment of society and help all sentient beings to achieve salvation. Renunciation and the ascetic life being restricted to monks, the laity was content to progress in this direction and found its saviours in the ecclesiastic structure and in its various embodiments like the Bodhisattvas, who postpone their own salvation to help alleviate the sufferings of other beings.

Though Buddhism spread to countries like Thailand, Burma, Sri Lanka, Japan, China and Korea, it is only in the northern Himalayas that we find such a large percentage of people who believe in mysticism, which is a peculiar feature of Mahayana Buddhism with its rituals, oracles and dances. This can be attributed partly to the extreme devotion of the people, their steadfast faith in the concept of karma and the belief that ultimate liberation comes through leading a monastic life.

♣ FACING PAGE: CHAM DANCERS PERFORMING AT KATHOK MONASTERY, EASTERN TIBET. CHAM DANCES ARE USUALLY THE RE-ENACTMENT OF SACRED HISTORICAL EVENTS OR ABOUT THE CONTINUAL TRANSFORMATION OF VOLATILE PSYCHIC FORCES.

Even today the visitor can see the Nechung oracle or the Nechung Dorje in Dharamsala that has acquired the name Little Lhasa.

COMMUNITY

In the Lamaist Himalayas, the system of Tsungral dictates that at least one son from every family take to asceticism so that the monasteries never lack in monks. Usually the elder son stays at home, marries, looks after the family property and continues the lineage while the younger son goes on to become a monk. In earlier times there was a law called the tra'a-trhe, which decreed that every family that could not send a son to a gompa pay a tax.

The outcome of this system was that a large number of young men donned the robes of a monk. The negative consequence of this system was that many able-bodied men were taken away from work in the fields or from other productive activities. It also led to the emergence of a large body of celibate women called chomos.

Parents also vow to send a terminally ill child to a gompa if their prayers are heard and the child is cured. People here do not view the act of sending a child to a gompa in economic terms but as a spiritual investment for the future.

Though Ladakh, Sikkim and Bhutan were monarchies—the last mentioned continues to

be one to this day—the gompa was the central institution. It dedicated most of the royal policies, exhorted the ruler to act with compassion and kept a check on royal absolutism. It was because of the monastic input into polity that there was a tendency towards non-violence or ahimsa, which is one of the main tenets of Buddhism. In this direction, the Tibetans were transformed from a warrior nation to one of the greatest pacific populations on earth which was the greatest tribute to Buddhism.

Being the largest institution in the Lamaist Himalaya, the gompas provide the main source of employment to lay people, hiring them as menials, artisans and agricultural labourers. Destitutes also flock to the gompa where they find a home and means of sustaining themselves. The gompas are a refuge for common people too, especially in times of

♣ BUDDHIST PRACTITIONERS GATHER TOGETHER AT THE MAIN PRAYER HALL AT KA-NYING SHEDRUP LING MONASTERY, NEPAL, TO RECEIVE TEACHING BY CHOKYI NYIMA RINPOCHE AND CHOLING RINPOCHE.

distress like famine. Years of frugality allowed the gompas to conserve the considerable wealth, received as donations from patrons and that which they generate through agriculture. The gompa larders are therefore always well-stocked and they never turn anyone away. This raises the status of the gompas in the eyes of the laity called minag-pa (worldly people). The monks maintain daily contact with the laity, which helps them in building up a close relationship. They use these opportunities to remind them of their great religious and cultural heritage. In their lectures, the lamas explain in simple terms abstract philosophical concepts, which help the people understand the essence of Buddhism. In their everyday interaction with the laity, the monks make clear to the common masses the subtle philosophical nuances of everyday phenomena like dreams and incidents which

cause perplexing moods. Many monks also go on to specialize in the study of medicine, astrology and painting that are practical and useful everyday.

In the isolated Himalayan region, religion forms the core of both the political and cultural life of the community. The only diversion for the people are the festivals and fairs which are organised under the aegis of the gompas and include dances, archery, horse-racing and feasting. The dancers are all monks who wear colourful masks. Even the dances have a religious flavour as they always end with the destruction of a ball or an effigy, symbolizing the victory of good over evil.

PATRONAGE

Ever since its inception, the Buddhist Sangha has thrived on the patronage of the laity. As monks are prohibited from owning any private property except for a set of robes and a few personal items, the common people provide them with their basic requirements of food, clothing and shelter. Every meal is supposed to be got by begging which is not considered derogatory at all. In fact the bhikku (one who has renounced the world) is highly respected in Buddhist society as a being whose existence goes beyond personal interests and for the reason that he has

♣ VENERABLE GELUKPA LAMAS ARRIVE AT KARSHA MONASTERY IN ZANSKAR, INDIA.

dedicated his entire life to the service of society.

At one point there was a debate over the eating of meat and the question was asked whether a monk could eat meat that has been offered to him. The Buddha replied that a monk could not eat meat deliberately, but if the meat was already prepared, he could consume it since there was no motivation on part of the householder or the monk in killing an animal. In Tibetan monasteries, the monks only eat the meat of dead animals since they did not play any part in the killing of that animal. Contribution to the Sangha is believed to earn merit for the donor because it is a noble deed and in keeping with the Buddhist tenet of karma, which preaches that present suffering is due to past actions. Many view this act of contribution as penitential. Apart from these deep religious convictions, the economic and social links of the community with the gompa also lead to patronage. Donations can be accepted by a lama but not in his personal capacity, only in the name of the Sangha. It

would come as a surprise to many outsiders that in the Lamaist Himalayas, people are not interested in accumulating money but are more interested in acquiring good karma that would help them achieve a better afterlife or even release them from the endless cycle of birth and death. In this direction we see that the nobility in the earlier days used to borrow large sums of money to pay for services in the gompas to accumulate good karma. Even today we see that a major part of the earnings of a family is donated to the gompa. Here we also see a rational element in the sense that since there are large donations to the gompa by the lay persons, they are in fact donating for the upkeep of the monks and the nuns who are their own brothers and sisters.

The earliest lay patrons of Buddhism were merchants and rulers who were wealthy enough to support this new religious institution. Ashoka, Songtsen Gampo and the Guge king, Lha-Lama Ye-She-O who patronised Lotswa Rinchen Zangpo are the most noted royal patrons. Another great name is that of the

Ladakhi king, Sengge Namgyal whose support led to the founding of Hanle gompa, Chemrey gompa and the world famous Hemis gompa, which is also the largest gompa in Ladakh.

Besides building gompas, these kings also bequeathed land and revenue to existing gompas and it is due to this that today the Hemis gompa ranks as one of the biggest landowners in Ladakh. As more and more people donated land to the gompas, they emerged as the leading landowners in the Himalayan region.

The common man too contributed in his own modest way, mostly in the form of regular gifts of cash and kind. Such gifts as food grain and beer are customary on special occasions like when a child is being admitted to a gompa. Each of these novices has a special cell called drah-shog, towards the upkeep of which the gompa owes no responsibility. This area is built and maintained by the novice's family for him to live in, cook and spend his initial years.

The Chinese occupation of Tibet in 1959 and the consequent flight of His Holiness, the Dalai Lama along with a hundred thousand of his followers led to the abandonment of many gompas in Tibet. In turn, new gompas sprang up in the Lamaist Himalayas and south India, built under the patronage of the lamas and the laity. The funding drive launched to build a gompa is called zinda, usually undertaken by the abbots. Most lay people contribute liberally and if the gompa is well known the subscription is more than enough to meet the demands of building and renovation.

Gompas like Hemis have many village gompas under their control and in times of need or on a regular basis the 'mother gompas' provide assistance to the affiliated smaller gompas. We can trace the origin of this system to the first

♣ MONKS BLOW LONG NARROW TRUMPETS AT THE SWAYAMBHUNATH STUPA, IN KATHMANDU, NEPAL.

gompa that was built in Tibet based on the model of the Vikramashila monastery of ancient India. Since then we have many gompas built on the models of earlier Indian monasteries and based on the unique traditions. During later times we see that many new gompas sprung up and these were affiliated to larger gompas—thus we have a chain of mother and daughter monasteries. It is also not uncommon for village gompas to be transferred from one 'mother gompa' to another for administrative and economic convenience. Poor economic conditions of the people and declining population are the main reasons for the deterioration and in some cases, abandonment of gompas.

The gompas have other sources of income too that explain the sustenance of this institution over long periods, often for centuries; for example, Hemis gompa in Ladakh has 51 villages under its control. Villagers helpless against the forces of nature like rain, snow and hail, which in times of harvest may mean loss of a whole year's hard work, engage lamas to perform the necessary rituals. On these occasions as well as in times of births and deaths, large offerings of cash, grain and butter are made. Some childless couples transfer their property to gompas in the hope of being blessed with a child. In some cases if a child is born handicapped, the family gives away their herds of yak, sheep and dzos (a hybrid animal, virtually indispensable in the Himalayas) to a gompa. There are others who opt to give away a part of their earnings. Even reincarnate lamas contribute their property to a gompa.

Patronage from the laity is needed for the everyday needs of the gompa, which include lighting of butter lamps, organizing food and fuel along with articles like incense for religious use.

♣ **LEFT:** YOUNG
MONKS ENJOY
A GAME OF
VOLLEYBALL
IN LINGSHED
MONASTERY,
LADAKH, INDIA.

Tsampa or roasted barley accompanied by tea is the staple food of the monks and meat an occasional luxury. The barley comes from land belonging to the gompas, which is cultivated by labourers. As all gompas are located in the remote high-altitude areas, we see that in these peculiar geographical conditions there is very little vegetation (except barley) and also a virtual absence of insects and pests. Furthermore, there is also a lot of solar radiation that destroys all pests. Under these conditions, barley can last for a very long time and unlike the villagers who use the excess barley for making chang (a popular alcoholic drink), the gompas store the barley for many years. This is one of the reasons why there was no famine in these areas even in times of bad harvest since the reserve stocks of barley could always be brought out for use to feed the hungry. The butter comes from the villagers and also from the nomads who, in addition to owning large herds, also maintain many of the yaks and dzos of the monasteries.

Every year the lamas go on a mission among the nomads to fulfill their spiritual and ritual needs, the latter being mainly the conduct of death ceremonies for those who have died in the previous year and to pray against forthcoming calamities and disasters. There are stories of nomads who had no route of escape in the vast grasslands in times of snowfall, as the animals could not run since there were no trees or shelter as far as the eye could see. The large herds could not be accommodated in the tents. In such a situation we hear of the animals huddled together with snow falling inch by inch and the animals slowly freezing to death. To ward off such situations the nomads believe in many good luck charms and amulets, specially dispensed by the lamas. All these amulets are believed to have been empowered by the spiritual power of the lamas and would hence protect them

♣ LEFT: MONKS LIGHTING BUTTER LAMPS AT SARNATH, INDIA.

♣ RIGHT: NUNS ENJOYING A CUP OF BUTTER TEA AT THE DORJE DZONG NUNNERY IN KARSHA ZANSKAR, INDIA. THE DORJE DZONG, OCCUPIES A HILLTOP TO THE WEST OF THE MAIN MONASTERY. THE RUINS AROUND THIS NUNNERY ARE BELIEVED TO BE THE ORIGINAL MONASTIC FOUNDATION OF KARSHA.

♣ PUCHANG
(CREMATION
PLACE)
OF URGYEN
TULKU RINPOCHE
IN NEPAL.

from all the evil spirits which sometimes manifest themselves in the dreams.

Trade has always been a source of prosperity for the monasteries. Many gompas situated on trade routes offered protection to nomadic caravans from bandits and thieves. Till recently, the greatest profit was in the salt trade, a cherished commodity in the Himalayas—salt, meat and animal products were brought by the nomads who exchanged them for articles of daily use.

Moneylending was another activity, the rate of interest being one-fifth of the amount lent annually. In times of bad weather or when crops failed and famine was imminent, barley was bartered. The villagers either replenish the gompas' stocks in the next harvest or exchange it for gold, silver and other precious metals.

The building of chortens (stupas) and the commissioning of thangkas (religious paintings) are thought to be by far the greatest acts of piety earning great merit. The Buddhist belief in 'the bigger the object, the greater the merit' led to the building of gigantic statues. Precious stones that have ritual significance and enhance the value of an art object are also extensively donated for chortens, thangkas and appliquéd banners.

It is only in commissioned works that we find the names of artists and the customary verse that runs along with the painting ('with the merits accruing from this…'), dedicating it to the memory of their patrons or requests that the donor or his kin may attain Buddha-hood. Appliquéd banners have become so famous that some senior lamas travel with their own

appliqué masters and masterpieces. Due to royal patronage and Spartan lifestyles, gompas can afford to channelize resources towards commissioning works of art, prayer flags, celebration of festivals and the installation of images.

Other contributions come from the laity on occasions such as fairs, held after the harvest, when the air is filled with joy and there is a feeling of prosperity all around. Losar, or New Year, is the most popular Buddhist festival in the Himalayas and falls around late February or early March. The end of a year and the beginning of a new one is believed to be a period of transition and causes apprehension

in the minds of the people. Many of them therefore perform rites or offer gifts to the gompas to chase away evil spirits.

Earlier, before the new year actually began, there used to be a ritual dance accompanied to the beat of drums and trumpets in the Potala Palace in Tibet; the lead dancer would come forward and in a symbolic gesture pour spirit from a skull into a cauldron of boiling oil. Evil spirits sketched on a piece of cloth suspended over the fire were thus neutralized. This festival is now replicated in all the Tibetan settlements outside Tibet.

Monlam Chenmo is the great prayer festival held a few days after the new year

♣ YOUNG MONKS INSIDE THE CHOKYI NYIMA RINPOCHE MONASTERY, NEPAL.

as a kind of annual rejuvenation of the Buddhist faith. Prior to 1959 this was held on the fifteenth day of the month of Losar to commemorate the philosophical victory of Buddha Sakyamuni over six Indian Brahmanical teachers in a debate. Well attended by monks, the Dalai Lama used to give discourses on the Buddha's previous lives and at dusk there was an inspection of the monks. Other important festivals include Saga Dawa, the anniversary of the Buddha's mahaparinirvana, or the Buddha purnima. It is interesting to note that the Buddha was born on a full-moon night, he attained enlightenment on a full-moon night and he also attained mahaparinirvana (means the final 'blowing out'; the word 'death' is not used) on a full-moon night. The birth anniversary of Guru Padmasambhava and the ascension of Tsong-kha-pa who dedicated his life to the reform of Tibetan Buddhism are other important Buddhist festivals.

♣ FREE IN BODY, MIND AND SPIRIT, THESE PLAYFUL YOUNG MONKS RUN IN THE COMPOUND OF GAMTSE MONASTERY IN BHOBJIKHE, BHUTAN.

♣ PRECEDING
PAGES 74-75:
THE BOUDHNATH
STUPA, JUST 5
KILOMETRES
OUTSIDE
KATHMANDU IS
ONE OF THE
OLDEST BURIAL
MONUMENTS OF
NEPAL. ALONG WITH
SANCHI STUPA IN
INDIA AND THE
SWAYAMBHUNATH
STUPA IN NEPAL,
THIS IS AN EXAMPLE
OF MAMMOTH
BUDDHIST
ARCHITECTURE.

gompa art and
architecture

The only pieces of architectural grandeur to survive centuries of human and natural vicissitudes in the Lamaist Himalayas are the gompas. Breaking the monotony of the barren landscape, they stand out elegantly and from a distance, seem to recede into the lofty clouds. Royal patronage resulted in the viharas becoming mahaviharas, stone constructions replacing the earlier brick and wooden structures. Nalanda, Vikramashila, Odantapuri and Dhanyakataka in India became renowned centres attracting students from far and wide. Monasteries in Sri Lanka, Burma, Indonesia and Tibet also began to be built on the Indian model of the mandala with the sanctum sanctorum in the centre, surrounded by rooms and marked off from the outside by a wall, symbolizing the boundary between the sacred and the worldly. The layout represented the universe with the temple at the centre and the four guardian deities at the four cardinal points. This model was followed at Samye, Tibet's first monastery, built on the lines of Odantapuri. The Sanskrit work *Saddharamasmurty Upasthana Sutra* provided the guidelines for construction.

This phase spanning from the 10th to the 15th centuries is the first period in the architectural history of Tibet during which the great scholar Rinchen Zangpo is said to have built about one hundred and eight temples in western Tibet. The number is probably a conventional one as only a few monasteries of the period survive today, the most famous ones being Tabo, Alchi and Lhalun. This was the period when the western Tibetan kingdom of Guge was at its height and included Ladakh,

♣ FACING PAGE:
A GELUKPA MONK IN DHARAMSALA, INDIA, GIVES FINAL TOUCHES TO A PAINTING OF THE KALACHAKRA, OR WHEEL OF LIFE.

♣ RUINS IN TOLING, TSAPARANG, IN WESTERN TIBET. TOLING IS A PART OF ZHANGZHUNG, A PRE BUDDHIST, NOMADIC CIVILIZATION IN THE DESERT REGION SURROUNDING MOUNT KAILASH. ALTHOUGH ONLY A FEW TRACES OF ITS PHYSICAL PRESENCE REMAIN, THE HISTORY OF ZHANGZHUNG HAS BEEN PRESERVED IN BOTH BON AND BUDDHIST TRADITIONS.

♣ A THANGKA DEPICTING THE VARIOUS INCARNATIONS OF THE BUDDHA. AT THE BASE ARE THE WRATHFUL DEITIES. TIBETAN BUDDHISM IS CHARACTERIZED BY THE PRESENCE OF NUMEROUS MALEVOLENT GODS WHICH ARE IN FACT BORROWED FROM HINDU TANTRISM.

Zanskar, Spiti, Lahaul, upper Kinnaur, Purang and Rutok. All these early monasteries bear striking similarities in layout and construction.

Tabo monastery in Spiti is the best example of the first phase of gompa architecture when the Indian style was followed. The main complex is on a flat ground with all the temples built in linear symmetry. The du-khang (assembly room) is at the centre and the temples are arranged at the cardinal points all facing eastward, except for the gon-khang (the room where ritual costumes, human skulls and fearful Tantric divinities are housed), the z'al-ma (anteroom) and the monks' cells which are definitely a later addition and therefore do not fit into the symmetry. A boundary wall marking off the sacred space encloses the entire complex. Huien Tsang, the famous Chinese traveller, described Indian monasteries as full of paintings and ornamental decoration and Tabo is no exception: its rich murals have also earned for it the title 'Ajanta of the Himalayas.'

The second period starts roughly around the 14th or 15th century; the changed socio-political conditions in Tibet and India dictated the architectural styles. This period saw the decline and destruction of monasteries in India due to Turkish invasions and the rise of local Hindu kingdoms. The denial of patronage to the Buddhist monasteries followed by pillage, loot and destruction saw the snapping of cultural links between Tibet and the Indian mainland. The Mongol invasions and the consequent rise of the Gelukpa sect into a powerful movement led to the fusion of religious and secular authority and the establishment of the institution of the Dalai Lama as the religious and temporal ruler of Tibet. Sectarian rivalry and the ascendancy of temporal affairs saw bitter conflicts as the theological

♣ TOP: RATNA SAMBHAVA— THE BUDDHA EMANATING HIS RAYS OF COMPASSION.

♣ BOTTOM: GREEN TARA FRESCO. THE TERM TARA REFERS TO PUPIL OF THE THIRD EYE, THE EYE OF WISDOM. THE CULT OF TARA WAS PROPAGATED BY DIPANKARA ASTHA.

centres of Tashilunpo, Ganden and Sera in central Tibet became militarily powerful. Gompa building reached its peak during this period. All the important monasteries came up during this time including the gompas of Phyang, Hemis, Thikse and Likir in Ladakh; Ki, Tangyud and Dhankar in Spiti.

The main feature of these gompas is their shift from flat ground to hilltops due to strategic reasons. It was a period of warfare and gompas were targeted, as they were the repositories of wealth. From the late 13th century onwards, all the new gompas were built on top of the hills where they would get a commanding position and could defend themselves. In such a setting, the symmetry of the earlier period is missing as constraints of space gave rise to multi-storeyed gompas. Temples, cloisters and cells are arranged asymmetrically with white sloping walls and block windows. But even here the mandala symbolism of symmetry is not entirely lost: the temples at the higher levels indicate their pre-eminent position. For instance the zimchung, the personal room of the head lama is placed at a vantage point on the upper floors.

The primary element of gompa architecture is the courtyard—the flat space used for

♣ ORIGINALLY THE
WATCH TOWER OF
PARO MONASTERY IN
BHUTAN, THE
WINDOWS TAKE
ARTISTIC FORM IN
SHADES OF WHITE
AND ORANGE.

communal gatherings, performances of dances—which forms the entrance to the temple. After passing through the circumambulation corridor which is lined with prayer wheels, one proceeds to the chapel, the lha-khang (the temple proper) and the du-khang (assembly room) via the portico which again symbolizes the link between the outside and the sacred inner sanctum. Rows of monks sit facing each other in the assembly room with the head lama or the leader of the ceremony perched on a raised platform to the right of the deity. Bowls of water and other offerings are kept on the altar. The image of the presiding deity is at the centre, flanked by images of other deities all of which are on the far end of the wall. The room of the head lama is located above, indicating his high status. The gon-khang (chamber of horror) is the secret chamber where the chief protective deity of the Gelukpas, Mahakala Vajrabhairava is enshrined. It is here that one finds masks, weapons and skulls which help in performing protective rituals. Only the priest is allowed entry into the gon-khang, that too after protective meditation to shield himself from the wrathful deities. The monks' cells are smaller rooms with provisions to store fuel and some shelves to keep utensils. The kitchens and storeroom are adjacent, with the kitchens containing enormous cauldrons in which tea is prepared.

Doorways or windows in the ground floor of the monasteries are very rare, to protect against the icy winds. The bricks are all sun-dried as good quality stones are not available. The columns and capitals of the gompas are richly decorated and in them one can notice the influence of Kashmiri and Nepali patterns.

Buddhist texts lay down rules for the selection of the site for building a gompa: the ideal setting

is on a hill with land sloping away from the monastery and containing water. All the monasteries of Sikkim, Bhutan and many of Ladakh, Kinnaur, Spiti and Lahaul also face east to allow exposure to the first rays of the sun. Monastic architecture all over the Tibetan cultural area is homogenous whereas the local architecture widely differs, driving home the point that the great tradition of the Lamaist Himalayas is essentially the same, whereas the little tradition is very different, being conditioned by local factors.

The stupa, or chorten was originally constructed to house the ashes of the Buddha. According to sacred Buddhist texts, the ashes of the Buddha were divided into eight parts among the eight great powers of north India. The original stupa where a part of the ashes are encased is the Rambhar stupa in Khushinagar (literally, the town of happiness). Later, relics of other Buddhist saints also began to be kept within it and this became a time-honoured practice. Apart from the reliquary function, the stupas also serve as a votive offering and as a memorial, marking the site of an event in the Buddha's life. We can see a large number of stones around the stupas in the Lamaist Himalayas since there are no flowers or any other offerings in this area. There are a large number of manuals on stupa architecture in Sanskrit and Tibetan which, unlike in India, standardized stupa construction. All over the Lamaist Himalayas and Tibet stupas are identical in shape and proportion and look as if they have all been made by the same architect, which is intriguing, given the fact the tools of measurement are very simple. Miniatures made of metal, clay, wood, stone, flour and butter are used for contemplative purposes.

The stupa is divided into nine parts based on the nav-tala or the nine-level system. This is a representation of the Buddha's body, which in turn represents the perfect human form. It also symbolizes in part the five primeval elements of which the universe is composed, with the square base representing earth, the dome representing water, the shaft fire, the crescent air and the circle symbolizing ether.

Every great gompa has a chorten in which is preserved the remains of the head lama or a senior lama. In addition there are clay tablets called tsatsa which serve as votive objects. Old books and manuscripts are also conserved here since it would be irreligious to burn or throw them away after they are in tatters. Chortens can be built everywhere, near gompas, on roadsides, outside forests. Chortens of massive proportions called kumbums (a hundred thousand images) can be visited by pilgrims who start from the bottom and climb up to the top. The climb symbolizes the pilgrims' ascent

in the universe and the deities at the highest level represent ultimate knowledge and revelation. The descent marks their return to the point of beginning. The inside walls of the chorten are painted with murals, each telling a different story that transports the visitor visually to a higher realm and is an effective medium of communication.

A unique feature of Tibetan art is the use of powerful colours that appear in alternating fashion and are not seen anywhere in the world. It evokes images of terrifying deities, wrathful yakshas (a class of demigods), great mothers, sacred mandalas and landscapes of paradise. Themes from Mahayana and Vajrayana Buddhism are plenty, the most common being Bodhisattvas who are portrayed as ideal men leading other creatures to liberation.

Tibetan art is dominated by rigid iconometry based on the nav-tala system according to which the ideal human being measures nine spans, each span representing a division of the cosmos. This perfect being is in turn seen as a representation of the cosmos in terms of proportion and harmony of all the parts. Besides Indian and Nepalese styles, Tibetan art also shows Chinese influences that did not emphasize iconometry as seen in the

♣ THE ASSEMBLY HALL OF A MONASTERY ADORNED WITH THANGKAS AND MASSIVE TRUMPETS. CALLED RADONG, THE SOUND OF THESE TRUMPETS IS BELIEVED TO BE THE PUREST FORM OF MUSIC.

visualization of the clouds, trees, birds and cliffs. It is the Chinese element which has given a certain amount of flexibility to Lamaist art. Over the years there has arisen a misconception that Tibetan art is a product of influences from abroad. The truth is very far from this, in the sense that traditional influences have blended with all the diverse influences to create a unique form of art. Of

particular mention is the topic of the harsh deities who are representatives of the collective responses of the Tibetan people to a very harsh environment.

Among the Buddhist countries, the Tibetan school has the maximum works of art. In addition to paintings and sculptures we find ritual objects like the vajra or the thunderbolt, an essential object in tantric rituals. Vajra is

with the symbols and motifs, which are mostly of Indian origin, but modified to suit Tantric philosophy. Symbols can be comprehended in the gestures, moods and drapery which are elements in themselves, but the individual meaning of each gesture is a part of the whole symbol of the painting or sculpture which ultimately represents the doctrine of sunyata. Propounded by Nagarjuna, it literally means 'the void' and is a very abstract concept. We see thus the position of fingers, each representing one particular style and meaning that helps us to identify the idea behind the art, as in the case of two palms resting one above the other signifying the sealing of a bond. This sealing of the bond represents the sealing of a secret doctrine. When unlettered people bow or make reverential gestures upon seeing the statues and paintings, it is evident that they are proficient in the non-verbal vocabulary of the deities.

Significantly, it is not the subject of art that decides its value in Buddhism but the inspiration it provides to the beholder. We can recount a great story from the life of the Buddha, taught to all the artists and one can see even today this story being repeated to all the students of Tibetan art. According to this story, an artist was commissioned to paint the face of Lord Buddha and when he had finished painting the body of the great master, he proceeded to paint the eyes and then realized that he could not concentrate on the eyes of the Master, as they were very overpowering. Realising his mistake, the painter saw the reflection of the Master in the water and then proceeded to paint. Whenever one visits the gompa, the exercise of viewing an object of art is always seen as a religious task; thus, the

translated into Tibetan as dorje and can either mean a diamond or thunderbolt, both of which signify indestructibility. Tibetan ceremonies take place to the accompaniment of ritual music. Even musical instruments are transformed into pieces of art, each with a symbolic meaning.

Lamaist art is highly philosophical and complex. To understand it, one must be familiar

♣ FOLLOWING PAGE 92: A MONK PRAYS INSIDE A SACRED SPACE AT BODHGAYA, INDIA.

elderly and the monks give the commentaries to the young. In the 19th century, there was a shift in terms of viewing Tibetan art in the great gompas with the advent of the Europeans, who called this art demonic. It had such a great effect that many of the images of these terrifying deities were then not shown to outsiders for fear of being ridiculed. It is only in recent years that this historical wrong has being corrected.

THANGKA PAINTING

Religious paintings are of three kinds: murals, manuscript illustrations and thangkas, the last being most popular as they can be easily rolled and carried. In ancient India patacitras, or scroll drawings, were effective methods of religious propagation supplementing oral preaching in ancient India. The stone sculptures at Sanchi stupa are shaped in the form of scrolls where the story of the Buddha's life is told. The patacitra tradition survives in India only in Orissa, but the themes are all Hindu.

Lamaism lays down stringent rules regarding proportion, thematic selection and consecration of thangkas and thus we see that we cannot find any thangkas that are incomplete or flawed. Most of them have patron monks and are generally hung in monastic shrines or in domestic altars as devotional objects signifying a sacred space in the home. Since a thangka is conceived as a mandala (universe in a microcosm), it is also used as a focal point for meditation. During festivals large thangkas are displayed on the slopes of a hill to offer the public a view. Thangkas depicting family life and tutelary

deities are carried by travellers and merchants. There is also a class of thangkas called lineage thangkas, which are kept in the monasteries and contain images of great teachers and departed monks.

A thangka is painted on a cotton cloth fitted in a bamboo frame to prevent folds. A mixture of glue and chalk is added to stiffen the cloth. Pigments from vegetables are mixed with resin and the outline is drawn first in black or red. Perforated stencils are used in case copies are required. The colours are filled in with a brush made of animal hair, preferably goat hair. The completed thangka is provided with a silk frame of red or yellow with two wooden rods,

which makes it a vertical scroll that is supposed to be rolled from the bottom upwards. It also has a protective silk cover with two coloured ribbons at the edge to keep it firmly rolled.

The symbolism of the mandala plan is duplicated in thangka paintings: a brocade patch at the bottom embroidered with a sky dragon symbolizes the doorway, and a tricoloured rainbow around the thangka represents the boundary between the sacred and the profane.

The main attraction of Tibetan painting is the sudden contrast in colours, provided by alternating reds, blues and greens. Gold is also widely used for details and as an outline. The

♣ DEATH FRESCOES INSIDE DRIGUNG MONASTERY, TIBET. DRIGUNG IS FAMOUS FOR ITS SKY BURIAL CEREMONY. SKY BURIAL IS A RELIGIOUS CEREMONY WHERE THE CORPSE IS BROKEN IN PIECES AND PLACED ON A DESIGNATED ROCKY CIRCLE IN THE SACRED BURIAL AREA, ALLOWING VULTURES, KNOWN AS DAKINIS, OR, SKY GODDESSES, TO CONSUME THE REMAINS.

outline fixes the space and enhances the painting's beauty by limiting the design and heightening the contrasts. Since the colours and proportions of the deities have to strictly follow the iconometric and iconographic rules, the only scope for artistic experimentation is in the background consisting of clouds, creepers and sceneries.

The gods are usually depicted in adamantine postures, holding the thunderbolt, which signifies adamantine truth, or in the meditative posture with hands in the gesture of blessing. Demoniacal deities break all forms of iconometry with protruding arms, swollen bellies, enormous teeth, fearful expressions and weapons in hand. Their frenzied appearance is in total contrast to the calm of the benevolent gods.

The colours used in the thangkas are divided into three categories: mild colours for the Bodhisattvas, slightly stronger colours for tutelary images and other creatures, and bold, dark colours like black and blue reserved for the terrifying deities.

Wall paintings also have subjects similar to thangkas, but are not as lavish as the latter and very little is known about them. The earliest wall paintings can be found in the monasteries at Tabo and Alchi, which are very similar to the famous Ajanta frescoes. Here there is a large-scale use of green and white colours and the figures are also drawn in the Indian or Indo-Greek (Gandhara) style.

Early Indian styles predominate with the Tantric concept of yab-yum, or the union of the male and the female being the most common symbols. Sadly, such statues and paintings, have been categorised in the popular mindset as vulgar. Far from being vulgar, these paintings are representative of a very abstract theme that is central to Vajrayana Buddhism. The union of the male and the female symbolises the path to attaining salvation with the male representing the mystic force and the female representing the wisdom thus overcoming the false duality of our existence. This is a concept that has its roots in the Indian Tantric tradition and was popular in both the

Buddhist and Hindu Tantras. These themes did not find full favour in China and Japan, and were not popular there. In Tibet the yab-yums were not displayed for general viewing, but only for people who were properly instructed.

Another popular set of themes from the *Jatakas* showing the Bodhisattvas in the earlier lives of the Buddha. Set in many places, including famous towns and jungles of ancient India, with animals, caravans, and magic featuring in the stories, they are very popular with children.

When we come to the mural we see that there is no attempt in the wall paintings to give a concrete vision of scenery, using mild colours like red and yellow, both of which are associated with renunciation. There was a shift in the content and approach towards thangka painting in the 13th century due to the decline of Indian influences on account of the destruction of Buddhist monasteries in India

after the rise of the Turkish invaders and the consequent snapping of ties with Tibet. There are more influences from China seen in the large-scale use of blue and red colour as also the use of clouds and sceneries. The figures are also treated in a Mongoloid fashion with elongated cheekbones.

Early Buddhist art portrayed the Buddha as a superhuman with strong limbs and a broad chest. This is evident in the sculptures of the Kushana period where the Buddha and the Bodhisattavas are shown as strong beings. With the growth in philosophy and the awareness of the importance of meditation, the deities began to be portrayed as gentle beings with drooping eyes or inward-looking eyes which symbolized inner peace, poise and a certain restraint. This phase is represented by the inward-looking eyes, which conveys the idea that a superhuman is one who has conquered himself and not the world.

The second phase in wall paintings, visible in later monasteries such as Ki, Phyang and Hemis, show clear Chinese influences. The rigid iconometry of the earlier period does not prevail and there is a remarkable fluidity, seen in the flowing robes. There is more ornamentation seen in the flowing, elaborate drapery, a greater emphasis on facial expressions and the vast blank spaces are filled with details taken from daily life along with composite flower motifs. It was believed that the use of costly materials would add to the prestige and earn spiritual merit, hence the excessive use of gold as a decorative element.

There is another class of thangkas called the medicinal thangkas where the Medicine Buddha or Sangye Menla is worshipped. In addition, many paintings also detail the various parts of the body and the flow of channels, techniques of treatment and various medicinal plants. During the earlier times when there was no cure for many diseases, the patients commissioned a special thangka for the Medicine Buddha to save them from illnesses.

Another theme in the thangkas is a focus on the great Indian and Buddhist masters. Normally in all the monasteries we can trace the history by looking at the great masters who graced the gompas. Their memory is preserved in the thangka paintings along with the monastic chronicles called the namthar.

MANDALAS

Abstract mandala painting reached its peak after the rise of the Gelukpas in the 14th century when new texts were composed. The mandala is a sacred circle surrounded by eight rays signifying an area purified of all transitory and dualist ideas. Far more numerous than any other work of art, they are symbolic representations of Buddhist deities. A mandala is also seen as a representation of the cosmos—the centre of the mandala is the centre of the universe created out of the germinal syllable of meditation and therefore contains a picture of a holy city or a famous temple.

The outer circle has a ring of brilliant flames called the mountain of fire which is supposed to deny access to the mysterious world within the circle. The flame symbolises consciousness, which consumes all ignorance and obstacles. The second circle shows the thunderbolt, representing pure consciousness. The third circle with eight cemeteries symbolises the eight consciousnesses, or the illusory world. A ring of lotus petals forms the next boundary—the harmonious unfolding of spiritual vision. Next we enter the mandala

proper with its four gates signifying the first stage of knowledge. Within these gates is the sacred city, the inner park of which has another four gates with symbols of the thunderbolt representing absolute power. At the centre is the primal force where the Buddha appears, surrounded by lotus flowers. Sand and wood are the preferred materials for making mandalas and they are usually kept for a certain period of time after which they are ritually destroyed. This final act is symbolic of the Buddhist notion of impermanence. As a meditational aid the mandalas help the devotee to concentrate. Stage by stage, the devotee gets to the centre and in this process he rids himself of all imperfections and enters the desired goal.

SCULPTURE

Buddhist sculptures are mostly in bronze and copper except for a few in stone and wood, since good quality stone was hard to find in the Himalayas and wood was not plentiful. The rules of iconometry and proportions were so strictly emphasized that each statue appears to be a replica of the previous one. Both the malevolent and benevolent deities are depicted in Buddhist sculpture. The main postures of the tranquil deities are vajrasana where the legs are folded with the soles inward and dhyanasana which symbolises emergence from meditation. The dharmachakra mudra represents the Turning of the Wheel, the sarana mudra

♣ TULSHIG RINPOCHE BLESSING BUDDHA STATUES IN BOUDHANATH, KATHMANDU, NEPAL.

symbolizes the refuge-giving attitude, and the blessing-giving attitude is indicated by the abhaya mudra. The most popular statues are those of Bodhisattva Avalokitesvara, his manifestation as Padmapani (holding a lotus) and Bodhisattva Manjusri. Sometimes Avalokitesvara is shown with four heads or with eleven heads, numerous pairs of hands and eyes on the palm, which show his concern for the welfare of other beings. Mahakala is the most common wrathful deity with a skull

in his hand, protruding tongue and large, terrifying eyes.

In the case of sculptures, we see a shift from the 13th century with the predominance of local influences and the decline of Indian influences as manifested in the Maitreya image. The Maitreya or Future Buddha is a very popular theme since it is believed that in times of crisis the Future Buddha would descend to the earth. In the monasteries of Ladakh, particularly at Thikse, one can see that the eyes of the Maitreya are treated with an epicanthic fold and the cheekbones are protruding giving an appearance of Mongoloid influence.

Another favourite subject is the yab-yum statue in various stages of copulation with only the back visible. The robe acting as a halo and the decorated pedestal heightens the effect. Ornamentation is used liberally and apart from bronze, copper and brass, silver and gold are also used extensively. Statues are first cast either hollow or solid and then gilded with precious metals. We also see that there are many statues that belong to a class of deities.

There is one room in the monastery, the gon-khang, which is always kept under lock and key. The translation as the chamber of horrors is a rather accurate description. Inside this room a large number of statues of the terrifying deities are open on special occasions to the monks who are initiated. It is in these deities that we see the wrathful character of the local cults. Some of them are called yi-dams or tutelary deities. A monk can choose any tutelary deity which is oriented towards a specific goal or a life term goal and some of the tutelary deities are the terrifying deities. Typically, the monk begins his day with a prayer to the tutelary deity with whom he identifies and then the deity offers the right guidance to proceed towards the goal. Since all human beings are not of the same mental disposition and are afflicted with anger, fear or sloth to various degrees, identifying with different terrifying deities helps to attain perfection.

In addition to sculptures, a number of devices like prayer flags and dorjes (thunderbolts) are extensively used in Tantric rituals along with a bell, all of which, when seen in the context of a monastery, recreate the experience of a vibrant Tantric Buddhist experience. The bell and the dorje signify emptiness and cognition with the act of penetration showing skilful means. Prayer wheels, drums, musical instruments and magic darts made of metal and human or animal bones are other ritual accessories. Prayer flags are extensively used during times of festivals when the whole occasion is joyous and the fluttering flags proclaim the presence of gods. In the barren landscape of Ladakh and the whole of the western Himalayas, there are many prayer flags fluttering as also many Mani stones engraved with the sacred mantra 'Om Mani Padme Hum,' translating as 'The Jewel is in the Lotus.' Mani, the jewel, symbolizes aspects of method, compassion and love, and the altruistic intention to become enlightened. Padme means lotus and symbolizes wisdom. Growing out of mud but not being stained by mud, the lotus indicates a quality of wisdom. The last syllabus, Hum, meaning inseparability, symbolizes purity that can be achieved by the unity of method and wisdom.

All over the Lamaist Himalayas we see many people from all walks of life, both young and old with prayer wheels constantly rotating in their hands, chanting the devotional mantra 'Om Mani Padme Hum'. Along with the prayer wheels, rosaries made out of 108 beads are used during the time of prayers. Beads are normally made out of wood or stones but there are some beads that are made of human bones and are rarely used except in esoteric rituals.

because their profession goes against the Buddhist ethic of non-violence. Surprisingly, many gompas showed a preference for students of aristocratic lineage but now the process has been terminated, as recruits are few.

After two to three years when a genen has passed the requisite examinations, he becomes a novitiate or da-pa. The tender age of seven or eight is usually too young for a boy to decide of his own free will, and the two years which he spends as a beginner help condition him to the new environment. Once he has passed the exams, the chief abbot, the khenpo or kusso asks him, 'Do you come of your own free will? Are you free from debts, deformities, diseases? Have you neglected the Three Commandments? Have you done any sin grave enough to cause loss of life?' Then enquiries about his parentage and residence are made. Only after getting satisfactory replies does the permission come. It is only the very obstinate and dull students who are weeded out; the vast majority stay on.

The purpose of enquiring into the parentage and banning debtors and slaves started during the period of the Buddha himself as he felt that they did not become monks out of conviction but sought to don the robes to end their miseries. The Buddha himself allowed women to enter the Order. In Mahayana Buddhism the nuns are called anis but the number of ani-gompas (monasteries for nuns) are few.

Once selected the da-pa is ceremoniously brought into the gompa dressed in his finest clothes which are then exchanged for the robes of the Order, in imitation of the 'Great Going Forth' of the Buddha. The da-pa has to observe

♣ A BOOM LAMA (TANTRIC ADEPT) OF THE TIBETAN BUDDHIST LAMA SECT, NYINGMA, ON HIS SEAT. A BOOM LAMA AND HIS FAMILY ARE THE MOST RESPECTED FAMILY IN THE HUMLA REGION OF NEPAL.

disable him from discharging his duties properly. If found to be satisfactory, the boy is taken into the monastery and his family makes presents of tea, beer and eatables. There is no elaborate ceremony, as the genen is yet to become a part of the gompa.

There is no caste system in Buddhism and a person belonging to any social group irrespective of his family status may aspire for monkhood. But certain classes of people like butchers and blacksmiths are deemed impure thirty-six rules. In addition to studying, he is engaged in menial duties like serving tea, food and cleaning rooms. Lay persons cannot serve the monks but only bring food and drinks for them till the doorway. The novice does this work for a period of three years, after which he passes out of the preliminary stage to that of the rig-chun.

In this stage the da-pa has a cell to himself and is relieved of the many menial jobs, but he is still not fully entitled to participate in the religious rites. The teacher liberally uses his cane during this period to instill in the novice an iron discipline.

The next stage is that of the gelong who is a fully ordained monk having to observe two hundred and fifty-three rules. It takes about twelve years of study to become a gelong, and it is usually at the age of twenty-five that a trainee completes this stage. A gelong literally means a 'virtuous or clerical beggar'. Entry into this stage is an occasion for celebration wherein the trainee is presented with a scarf, signifying respect and authority. Being a fully ordained monk does not entitle the gelong to advance to the next position of assistant abbot, which can only be held by a person qualified as a Geshe-Lha-rampas. This is one of the changes made by His Holiness the 13th Dalai Lama to uphold the dignity of the post.

At the apex of the monastic hierarchy is an abbot or khenpo. This post is an elected one and held usually for a period of six years. In Tantric monasteries the assistant abbot automatically becomes the abbot after a three-year term and earns the title of rinpoche. At the end of his three-year term he retires and becomes an abbot emeritus (kanzur rinpoche)

♣ FACES OF A KIND APPEAR IN DIFFERENT FRAMES OF MIND—GENENS, OR ABBOT MONKS IN LINGSHED MONASTERY, LADAKH, INDIA.

and may either continue teaching as a guru, go for a formal Tantric meditational retreat, or go into the mountains to retreat in seclusion. A monastery can also be headed by a kusso (or kushok) who is an incarnate lama. A kusso can head a monastery after undergoing long and rigorous training in the theory and practice of Buddhism. A kusso is regarded as equal to a tulku, also an incarnate lama. The term 'lama' is often used indiscriminately and loosely for all monks but strictly speaking the term is reserved for incarnate lamas who are regarded as living Buddhas/Bodhisattvas, gurus who give discourses, or for Geshes (spiritual preceptors).

The most famous among the incarnate lamas are the Dalai Lama and the Tashi Lama, also called the Panchen Lama. The institution of the Dalai Lama was started in the 15th century and the Dalai Lama is regarded as the reincarnation of the Bodhisattva Avalokitesvara, known in Tibetan as Chenrezi, the patron deity of Tibet. Below the Dalai Lama is the Tashi Lama and below him come numerous reincarnate lamas who are believed to be embodiments of Indian and Tibetan saints. Nunneries too have female reincarnations of goddesses who are appointed as abbesses of monasteries.

According to the Buddhist theory of reincarnation, when a lama dies, his spirit enters the soul of an infant who is born a few days after the lama's death; such children are identified with the help of oracles. Many infants who show signs of extreme intelligence are brought to the monastery by their parents and subjected to a test wherein articles of the deceased lama like prayer wheels and rosaries along with many duplicates are placed before

♣ THE 14TH DALAI LAMA CONFERRING THE KALACHAKRA INITIATION IN SARNATH, INDIA. BECAUSE OF ITS PROFUNDITY, THE KALACHAKRA INITIATION CAN ONLY BE BESTOWED BY THE MOST REALIZED OF TIBET'S LAMAS.

♣ FACING PAGE: HIS HOLINESS THE 14TH DALAI LAMA AT BODHGAYA, INDIA.

the child. The blessed child selects the items which were the personal possessions of the late lama. In rare instances, a lama may even indicate the place and the family in which his reincarnation will take place, but this is very rare. Normally it takes two to three years to find a successor but there have been cases where the reincarnation has not been identified for over ten years or where the whole lineage has come to an end.

There was, for instance, a case of a man in western Tibet who frequently saw visions of a distant land in his dreams. So obsessed was he with the monastic way of life far removed from his own, that he was convinced he belonged somewhere among the monks. As chance would have it, a delegation of monks from a Mongolian monastery who were on the move for many years in search of the reincarnate soul for their monastery found their candidate in this particular young man.

Early Buddhist monasteries did not have servants but the vast variety of tasks which had to be performed necessitated the induction of lay people, mostly for menial jobs. The abbot is helped by a number of officers with carefully delegated duties as follows: the lob-pon is the professor and an ordained monk who regulates the Vinaya rules. The cag-dso is the treasurer or the cashier who manages the economic transactions of the gompas. The ner-pa, also called spi-nyer, is the steward who handles the day-to-day work of the gompa. He shoulders the maximum responsibilities including redressing the grievances of lay menials. The ge-ko is in charge of law and order and is assisted in his duties by the hag-ners, who are orderlies. His is a prestigious post considering the fact that he is presented with a scarf. Another higher official is the um-dse, or the master of ceremonies. The ku-ner is responsible for the care of the holy books and other movable properties of the monastery. The gzim-dipon is the chamberlain and along with the mgon-gna-chen, the warden, who is in charge of hospitality; the tsi-dpon is the keeper of accounts. Other officials include the chabdren, who is responsible for supplying water, the jama who serves tea and the cook called the gsol-dpon.

Some of the larger gompas have officials like tax collectors, doctors, painters, merchant-monks and exorcists who are not found in the smaller monasteries. Strict discipline is observed in the gompas and there is a confession every fourteen days. The inmates of the gompa are divided into various clubs and minor offences are dealt with within the club,

punished by verbal chastisement. Offences like breaches of etiquette in sitting, walking, eating and gesturing are punished with ten strokes of the cane. The act of beating is executed by an official called the tab-gyug. Alternatively, the offender bows before the congregation and apologizes, wherein he is spared the rod.

Celibacy is one of the major monastic laws which is frequently broken, and along with the sins of murder and theft, it invites expulsion. Many of the monks who leave the Order are accused of such crimes and it is not always others who report on the lapsed monks. Often it is the monk's own conscience which prompts him to confess, even though he knows he may be defrocked and abused as ban-lok or

turncoat, and made to suffer social and personal disgrace for the rest of his life. If a defrocked monk has any technical or artistic training such as painting, he has a chance to eke out a living but many of them become wanderers or escape to seek refuge in some obscure place.

A monk's day begins before sunrise. The great conch shell signals the wake-up call for the first assembly, after which tea is served. There are five assemblies in a day till seven in the evening. During the day the monks perform their allocated services. The junior monks revise what they have read and after eating supper, which is served after the last assembly, they retire to bed.

♣ BON LAMAS IN PRAYER AT GOMPHU MONASTERY IN MUSTANG, NEPAL. THE BON TRADITION IS OLDER THAN BUDDHISM AND IS THE ORIGINAL AND AUTHENTIC RELIGION OF THE TIBETAN PEOPLE.

gompa and
education

Buddhists place a high premium on education. According to Buddhist philosophy, the root cause of man's suffering is desire and his helplessness is due to his inability to understand the cycle of birth and rebirth which in turn is due to his ignorance. Dispelling ignorance is the key to understanding the ways of the universe. Ancient India had developed the guru-shishya parampara where young students lived with their teachers, serving them while learning. The Buddhists took off from this point and the viharas or monastic residences became educational centres wherein the subjects of study were systematized. In the later centuries, with royal patronage from Buddhist and non-Buddhist rulers like the Guptas (3rd-5th century BC) and Harsha (606-647 AD) and the growth in commerce which increased the need for literate persons, the viharas changed character. They could now concentrate more on education as their basic needs of food, clothing and shelter were well looked after.

The viharas became mahaviharas or universities where subjects ranging from pure philosophy, grammar, language and psychology to medicine, astronomy and civil engineering were taught. The most famous among them was the Nalanda University which had its own seal bearing the inscription Sri Nalanda Mahavihariya Aryabhikku Sangharya. Other centres of education included Odantapuri, Valabhi, Dhanyakataka and Vikramashila which produced the corpus of Buddhist literature and more importantly, attracted students from far-off lands, including Tibet. These students went on to establish similar centres in the Himalayas. Rinchen Zangpo, the

✤ FACING PAGE:
RITUAL DRAWINGS OF FLOUR, BELIEVED TO DRIVE AWAY EVIL, ARE MADE ON SPECIAL OCCASIONS LIKE THE ANNUAL FESTIVAL.

♣ FOLLOWING PAGES 116-117: YOUNG NOVICES MEMORIZING THE SCRIPTURES AS PART OF THEIR CURRICULUM. THE EARLIEST BUDDHIST TEXTS WERE XYLOGRAPHED ON BIRCH BARKS WHICH ARE PRESERVED IN MANY OF THE MONASTERIES.

♣ AS MONKS CONCENTRATE ON THEIR SCRIPTURES, ONE NOVICE PEERS UPWARDS. MODERN MONASTIC TEACHING CONTINUES TO FOLLOW THE TRADITIONAL PATTERN—ALONG WITH SCRIPTURAL EDUCATION, EMPHASIS IS ALSO LAID ON ETIQUETTE, PRESENTATION, SPEECH, DEBATE, LITERATURE AND PHILOSOPHY.

famous Tibetan translator was one such student-visitor.

The text *Pali Mahavagga* tell us that an upadhyaya (spiritual guide) and acharya (teacher) admitted a pupil under them and became his spiritual guide while the student looked upon them as his father. Education was on the Vinaya, the *Jatakas* (a collection of five hundred stories from the earlier lives of the Buddha), hymns and the fundamental doctrines of Buddhism. Along with education emphasis was laid on etiquette which continues even today.

Modern monastic teaching continues to follow the traditional pattern. In the first stage, the beginner is taught the alphabets and made to recite some basic Buddhist texts, including prayers for general welfare and confession of sins. The correct form of presentation and the idea behind it are given importance for which the student is taught proverbs and the manner of presentation. Called the four principles of speech, the texts say, 'It (speech) should be vigorous or it will not enlighten and more importantly it must end suitably otherwise its effect will be lost; it should be bold as a lion, gentle and soft as a hare, pointed as an arrow and evenly balanced as a thunderbolt. Similarly speech should be connected and not disparate.' The beginner is also taught to avoid negative actions and emotions. These initial years are instrumental in shaping the personality of the probationer to prepare him for the monastic ideal.

The next stage is that of the novitiate or the da-pa. A ceremonial tonsure initiates the da-pa into the monastic order though not as a full member. The preliminary phase lasts for three years during which the student has to pass two examinations, the first of which is held within a year. The main subjects taught are the Vinaya, the Sutras and the drawing of mandalas (geometric patterns of squares, circles and triangles illustrating abstract concepts of the Buddhist cosmology) which is unique to Mahayana Buddhism. For the first examination the syllabus consists of books which detail the three magic circles of the Tathagatha (a title for the Buddha: One Who has Come and Gone Thus), the Avalokitesvara and finally the circle of the demoniacal. The examination lasts for three days and the candidate has to stand before an assembly and recite the texts with the help of a prompter. Most students need a second attempt to pass but for those who fail repeatedly there is no other option but to leave.

The da-pa also spends a lot of time practising calligraphy, as Tibetans are passionate about this. There is also some exposure to arts and crafts such as painting and ritual cake-making and those who show a special inclination to pursue careers in that direction are encouraged to do so. Such students are granted special privileges like exemption from menial duties and an independent cell, provided they pass the two basic examinations.

For the second examination which is held after a gap of two years, the da-pa has to memorize more texts which are divided into five groups namely: *Namdrel*, the study of logic, *Parchin*, a comparative study of Buddhist scriptures, *Oumak*, which teaches the avoidance of extremes, *Dzo*, dealing with metaphysics and *Dulwa*, where the Vinaya (canonical law) is taught. The second examination is similar to the first one but more prestigious. After passing this, the novice is

♣ A YOUNG MONK PRAYS ATOP THE JHOKHANG ROOF, LHASA, TIBET.

presented with a silk scarf and accepted into monkhood. But even at this stage he is not thought to be mature enough to discuss grave topics of philosophy with his master.

The curriculum is for thirteen years in which specialized and complex texts are taught, a rigorous academic regimen follows

♣ A YOUNG GELUKPA
NOVICE TAKES
TIME OFF HIS
RELIGIOUS ROUTINE
TO LIVE HIS
CHILDHOOD.

and debates and examinations are held. At the end of thirteen years the monks receive the degree of geshe. Though this was first started by the Sakya school, after the reforms of His Holiness the 13th Dalai Lama, stringent conditions were laid down and the whole process systematized.

Tibetan Buddhism pays special attention to debate as it helps sharpen the intellect and analytical faculties, enabling the monks to swim through the cross currents of logic and grasp reality. Debate forms a part of the monk's daily routine and so high is the level of proficiency that he can argue a single point in fourteen different ways. An outsider who enters a gompa when a debate session is on is shocked to find monks adopting aggressive postures and

seemingly on the verge of violence. But they are merely assuming traditional postures which resemble gestures of martial arts. Each posture has a specific meaning and is symbolic. The victor in a debate is carried around the gompa on the opponent's shoulders. The purpose is not to humiliate the loser but to make him realize his misconception, and obtain a thorough knowledge of the doctrine by fielding questions from obscure viewpoints to improve his presentation.

Literature studied by the monks is predominantly religious, the principal ones being the *Kangyur* and the *Tangyur*, Tibetan Buddhist canonical works that explain in great detail Buddhist dogma, philosophy and precepts. Biographies, or namthar (liberation) of saints are also popular. Another class of literature are the writings of the great Guru Padmasambhava which are hidden in caves and revealed occasionally. This is a special feature of the Nyingma sect. There are a large number of works on tantric themes in the Nyingma sect whereas the Geluk sect emphasizes the sutras or the teachings. This difference is not only textual but is also connected with the method. Tantric methods offer a scope for immediate understanding, whereas the Geluk and the other reformed sects offer a path that is mediated. Special mention can be made of the practice of tummo by which heat is generated inside the body and also the dzogchen meditation that is a speciality of the Nyingmas.

Besides these there are works on secular topics like the *Vaidurya Karpo* on astronomy, the *Vaidurya Yasel* concerning astrology and the *Vaidurya Ngonpo* dealing with medicine. By far the most important work on medicine is the *Rgyud-bzhi* which is a literal translation of the *Astanga Hridaya Samahita* an ancient Indian medicinal text. Monks who study to become doctors are called amchis and their whole course of study lasts for 13 years, during which a greater part of the study is spent on acquiring proficiency in the area of pulse analysis. This is particularly important, as the Tibetans believe that there are three pulses, initial, medial and neutral and a proper diagnosis is needed. In keeping with the Buddhist tradition, there is an emphasis on compassion and psychology and all diseases are believed to have a psychosomatic base. Firstly there are three humors in the body and an imbalance of the three disrupts the srog or life energy and must hence be corrected. Taking medicines and proper bodily habits can

♣ A YOUNG NUN CARRIES A CHILD ON A SNOWY DAY IN THE HUMLA REGION, NEPAL.

help correct the imbalances. Furthermore, it is believed that all human beings live in three worlds simultaneously, the pragmatic world of everyday life, the world of karma where we think about the good and the bad actions and dharma orientation, or the future afterlife. When there is disharmony in our life patterns, there is a disruption of the life energy that manifests itself in bodily disorders. Therefore in addition to medicines, the amchis also ask the patients to perform rituals as they cleanse the mind of the devotee.

There are also manuals on architecture and sculpture and pilgrimage guides. When Buddhism was introduced to Tibet in the 7th century AD, the earliest batch of Tibetan Buddhists came to India to study in the flourishing universities of Nalanda, Odantapuri and Dhanyakataka. Apart from the Buddhist religion, subjects like medicine, astrology, astronomy and iconography also attracted many students. This multifaceted character of the Indian monasteries was adopted by the Tibetan gompas. They borrowed from Indic sciences and developed them into sophisticated systems by integrating them with earlier practices against the background of Buddhist cosmology.

The other Indian sciences that became popular were astrology and astronomy as both attempt to explain the unknown and their effects on humans. Buddhists fervently believe that in addition to past actions or karma, the movements of planets and spirits also influence one's life. These branches of study involve complex calculations of planetary positions and the spirit associated with them. The basic astro-science text, the *Kalachakra Tantra*, translated from Sanskrit in 1027 AD, delves deep into the origins of the universe, its

♣ ANI (BUDDHIST NUN) TENZIN WITH TWO YOUNG DISCIPLES, SWAYAMBHUNATH, KATHMANDU, NEPAL.

♣ FACING PAGE: THE JONANG KUMBUM, IN THE REMOTE PHUNTSOLING VALLEY OF TIBET ONCE HOUSED THOUSANDS OF SACRED IMAGES OF THE BUDDHA'S TEACHINGS. BLASTED BY DYNAMITE IN 1959, THIS ONCE MAGNIFICENT TEMPLE IS STILL EERILY IMPOSING.

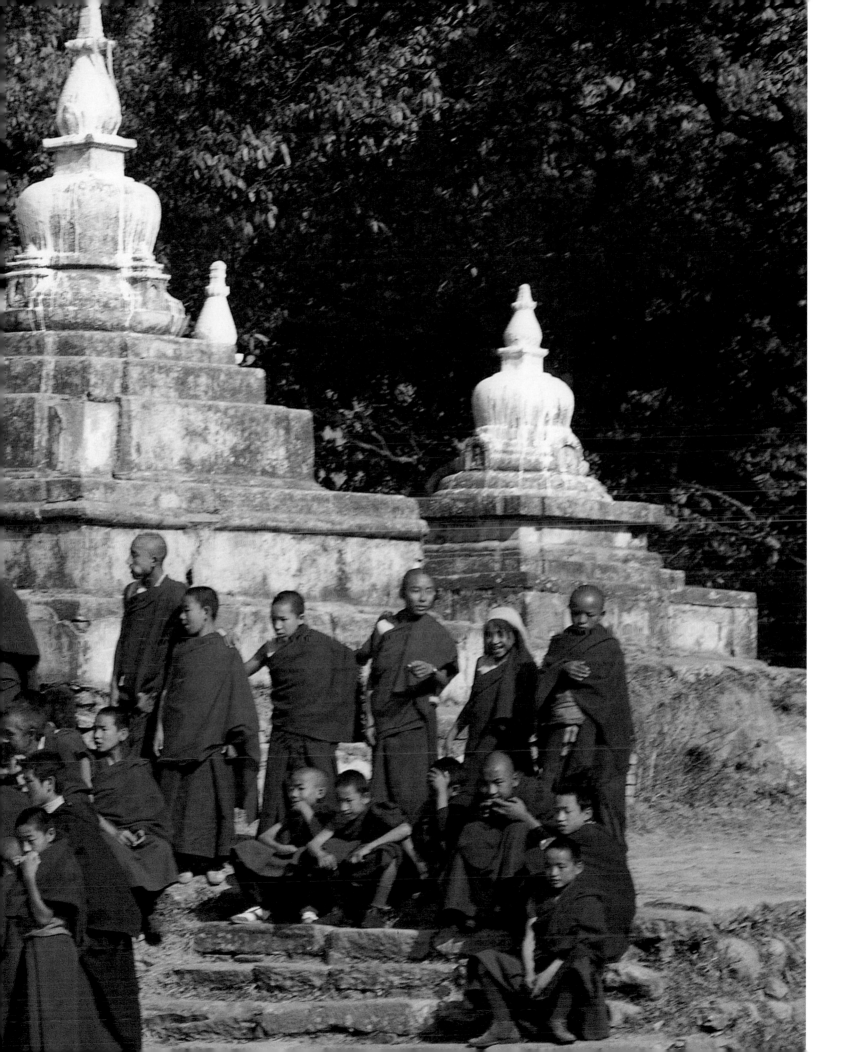

cosmology, movements of the planets and the five elements.

The Tibetan lunar calendar is organized in cycles, each represented by an animal. These are combined with the five elements, so each year is a combination of an element and an animal: Iron-Sheep, Earth-Sheep and so on. In a sixty-year cycle called rapchung, some years are considered lucky and others are unfavourable due to astral influences.

Most people consult lamas to cast horoscopes, marriage and medical charts and to predict the time of birth and death. Antidotes to ward off ill luck vary from performing rituals and giving alms to elaborate exorcist rituals.

The practice of rolance or warding off the messengers of the God of Death is one such interesting ritual, found only in the Spiti Valley. Relatives of the sick make an effigy of wood, plaster it with ground barley paste and paint it to make it lifelike. The figure is then adorned with gold and the scriptures read out. The objective is to enact a mock funeral to mislead the messengers of the God of Death. The gold goes to the monks and the effigy is cut into pieces and burnt. A special person is even appointed to proclaim that the sick man has been dead for nine long years, so the messengers are driven away forever.

♣ YOUNG MONKS CHANTING SCRIPTURES, MAHABUDDHA VIHARA MONASTERY, CLEMENT TOWN, INDIA.

CHAPTER SEVEN
famous
gompas

Guru Ghantal gompa: Majestic on a picturesque precipice with the Chandrabhaga river flowing below, this is one of the oldest Lahaul monasteries. The two-storied structure is devoid of any decoration except for some stray carvings or mandalas, but the monastery arouses interest because Guru Padmasambhava is said to have meditated here before journeying to Tibet. Since he was known as the second Buddha, Guru Ghantal is also called Gandahola (the second Bodh Gaya). The gompa contains an image of goddess Kali—such goddesses were incorporated into Buddhism during Guru Padmasambhava's time. Unfortunately, major repairs undertaken here in 1959 have only added to the architectural confusion of the complex.

Hemis gompa: The biggest gompa of Ladakh, Hemis is about forty-four kilometres from Leh on the Leh-Manali Road. Built in the 1630s under the patronage of Sengge Namgyal, it is the largest landowner in Ladakh. The quaint and serene Hemis hides behind it a turbulent past: Zorawar Singh of the Dogra Regiment attacked the monastery but the head lama saved impending disaster by paying a huge ransom. There was another crisis in 1956 when the chief lama disappeared, never to be seen again. Hemis remained without a head for twenty years till 1976 when a twelve-year-old was enthroned.

Hemis gompa is known the world over for its two-day annual festival, which unlike most other gompas, is held in the summer. Banners flutters on long poles erected in the courtyard and lamas in richly brocaded gowns and sporting

♣ FACING PAGE: RINGED BY THE ZANSKAR RANGE, KARSHA DEFIES THE DOMINATING PRESENCE OF THE MOUNTAINS. THIS 16TH-CENTURY GELUKPA MONASTERY WEARS A NEW LOOK AS IT HAS BEEN RENOVATED RECENTLY.

grotesque masks dance around them. Dancers dressed as skeletons come in occasionally to give a comic touch. The festival is dedicated to Guru Padmasambhava and at the end of the first day, an effigy made of barley is ritually cut into pieces signifying the destruction of the apostate king Lang Darma.

Hemis has a valuable collection of thangkas of which that of Guru Padmasambhava is note-worthy. Huge, embroidered (not painted), and embellished with pearls, it is open to viewing only once in twelve years. The last sighting was in 2004.

Kanum gompa: Far away in Kinnaur, India, Kanum is a favourite with Tibetologists. Alexander Cosimo de Koros, the renowned Hungarian Tibetologist spent three years studying the one hundred volumes of *Kangyur* and two hundred and fifty volumes of *Tangyur* preserved here. Both these texts are in such good condition that it is hard to believe their antiquity. These volumes were originally block-printed at the famous Narthang printing centre near Lhasa in 1820. The complex itself has seven big and small temples and a huge statue of the Buddha.

Ki gompa: A Gelukpa gompa, in Spiti, founded around the 11th century, Ki has been the subject of extensive research. The new structure is a modern day pigeon-hole stacked one above the other, but standing on the top floor, one can actually experience a feeling of complete detachment.

The monastery's basement contains among other things, a considerable cache of arms. Ki's history gives the explanation: situated on the prosperous trade route, it grew to be one of the richest gompas of the region and attracted the Mongols in the 17th century. It also saw the Kulu-

Ladakh wars, the Dogra Assault in 1841 and the Sikh Assault. Nature too took its toll during the 1975 earthquake.

Ki's main attractions for tourists are the beautiful thangkas depicting Sakyamuni and murals illustrating episodes from the *Jatakas*.

Lamayuru gompa: Along with Alchi and Likir, Lamayuru is the oldest gompa in Ladakh. Though tradition has it that it was founded by Rinchen Zangpo, according to some historians this was earlier a place of Bon-chos or animistic practices. Lamayuru adheres to the traditional mandala plan of a central temple surrounded by four temples in the four cardinal points.

However, only the main temple survives today.

Lamayuru also belongs to the Drigungpa sect and owes its wealth to King Jamyang Wangyal who donated vast tracts of land to it. Like Phyang, this too has an area called thampa ling (freedom land) where people convicted of crimes would not be punished.

The murals at Lamayuru are not very impressive though there is a mandala of fierce divinities in yab-yum (cosmic union) posture. In the inner shrine is a modern set of twenty-one manifestations of Tara in copper, crafted in Aligarh. There is also a chorten moulded in coloured butter, which is a special art of the lamas. This ancient art survives even today and butter sculptures are made during the annual festival held in March.

Likir gompa: Situated at the head of the small village of the same name in Ladakh, Likir was founded probably in the 12th century and belonged to the Kadampa order. Like many Kadampa gompas, this too became a Gelukpa gompa in the 15th century when the latter became the dominant sect in Tibet. The original structure was destroyed in a fire and the present building is an 18th-century structure.

Though neat and well maintained, Likir has little to offer visitors. There are images of Sakyamuni, Tsongkhapa and Maitreya along with clay images of the Buddha describing his life story and that of the sixteen arhats (saints). It is, however, famous for earthen pots which are in great demand. At present there are a hundred and twenty lamas here and it is they who conduct the rituals at Alchi.

Nako gompa: Nako belongs to the Dug-pa order, a total of four temples making up the complex. Though it escaped the invaders, the earthquake of 1975 shook the foundations of the four structures. There was also large-scale pillaging by vandals who removed the gold used extensively in the murals, stripping them bare.

The gompa situated in Spiti, still has a collection of carved images of deities like Vairocana, Amogasiddhi, Vajrasathava and Amitabha. Though small, the minute detailing captivates the viewer. The mural paintings are all of tutelary deities which were co-opted from the animistic practices in the Buddhist pantheon.

Phyang gompa: This famous gompa was built by the Ladakhi king, Jamyang Namgyal. According to the local legend, while digging a canal near Hemis, the workers came across a strange-looking lizard, which they killed without any thought. The king immediately fell ill and none of the royal physicians could cure him. As a last resort the king sent for Denma Kunga Trakpa, a mystic living in the Kailash-Mansarovar region. After much persuasion he restored the king's health. Later when Denma expressed the desire to start a monastery at Phyang, the king gave his complete support.

Today, the gompa is the main centre of the Drigyung-pa sect in Ladakh. It has three temples, rich with icons of the Buddha in his various poses. One of the interesting features

here is the flagstaff atop an elaborate pedestal: it is said that during the days of monarchy, if an offender managed to escape and reach this pole, he would be set free. The pillars of the temple are covered with tiger skin, a gift by the Kalon (premier) to Jamyang Namgyal.

Rangdum gompa: Situated in Zanskar, Rangdum is remote even by Ladakhi standards. The gompa was founded in the 18th century by the then ngari rinpoche (the head lama) under the patronage of Tshewang Namgyal. The large assembly hall or dukhang has statues of Avalokitesvara, Amitabha and Vairocana and in the entrance hall are brightly painted guardian divinities. The most striking mural is inside the zimchung (personal room of the head lama) and depicts the mythical land of Shambala with its armies in hot pursuit of

the enemy forces. Shambala is a yet to be identified land that is believed to prop up a warrior in times of crisis. The other attraction is the butter sculptures in the main hall.

Sankar gompa: Just three kilometres from Leh, this modern monastery is the daughter house of the Spituk gompa. In fact the head of Spituk, the venerable Kushok Bakula resides here. The icons here are made of pure gold and the wall paintings, as in any other gompa, depict scenes from the Panchatantra.

Shey gompa: According to tradition, Shey was the capital of Ladakh from ancient times, but history mentions it only in the 15th century, when King Lhachen Smal Gigum built a palace here. The gompa is on the summit of a hill and unlike most others which have a cluster of trees dramatically altering the stark mountain landscape, Shey has a group of chortens.

The main attraction here is the seven-and-a-half-metre-high copper statue of the Buddha commissioned by Deldan Namgyal, Sengge Namgyal's son. Copper mined from Lingshed and other villages around Ladakh was hammered into individual parts and brought together and gold weighing over five kilograms was used for plating. In front of this statue are numerous lamps, one of which is capable of holding enough butter to last a year. Near the palace at Shey one can see the funerals on the hilltops. After the ceremonies are performed at the house, the body is placed in a covered sedan chair and carried by a procession of lamas and commoners. It is then placed in a tubular walled oven and prayers are chanted during the course of the funeral. The ashes are scattered in a river later. Shey also has an oracle reader who comes on horseback during

the Shey Suhublas festival in August. After a three-day prayer this layman goes into a trance. The locals say that if one disbelieves the oracle's predictions and goes to another oracle, no answer will be given.

Spituk gompa: About seven kilometres from Leh on the right bank of the Indus, Spituk is not visible from a distance. It was founded in the 11th century and converted into a Gelukpa gompa in the 15th century. Here one can see the twenty-three manifestations of Tara in

♣ IN THE ZANSKAR VALLEY, THE LAND AROUND LINGSHED GOMPA IS SPECTACULARLY PRESERVED WITH ITS NATIVE CULTURE STILL INTACT, AS IT HAPPENS TO BE ONE OF THE MOST REMOTE PLACES IN THE WORLD.

♣ HEMIS GOMPA, LADAKH, INDIA, IS HOME TO ONE OF THE LARGEST THANGKAS IN THE WORLD. EXHIBITED ONCE IN TWELVE YEARS, IT WAS LAST SHOWN IN 2004.

addition to many icons of the Buddha. The most awe-inspiring is the image of Mahakala with thirty-five pairs of arms and eight pairs of legs. The face is covered with a scarf throughout the year and is revealed only in January during the annual festival. The wall paintings featuring skulls and skeletons are equally terrifying.

Stok gompa: Situated in Ladakh, the main attraction in the gompa complex is the Stok Palace. The monastery itself is not impressive but the palace has been converted into a museum and attracts visitors. It has sixty-five chambers of which the queen of Ladakh occupies eight. The museum is home to many treasured thangkas including a set of thirty-five representing the life of the Buddha. Painted in the 16th century, each of them has the handprint of King Tashi Namgyal on the obverse, as if certifying to their authenticity. Chinese influence is predominant in the thangkas: the background shows clouds with a profusion of blue and white. The museum also has a volume of scriptures lettered in gold. Another attraction here is the archery contest, held in July. Stok also has an oracle.

Tabo Chos Khor: Founded in 996 AD at Spiti, Tabo is the biggest and the oldest surviving monastery in India; it celebrated its 1000th anniversary in 1996 when His Holiness the Dalai Lama initiated the Kalachakra ceremony.

Tabo is built in the traditional Indian mandala pattern where the central temple is surrounded by other rooms. The original structure was destroyed in an earthquake in 1975 and in its place stands a modern modest shrine, home to about fifty lamas. A visitor to Tabo does not have much to see, the complex is dimly lit—the only way sunlight can enter is through a slit in the ceiling. For the serious Tibetologist, however, there is literally a holy mess of books and scriptures to wade through.

Tashiding gompa: The second most important monastery of Sikkim, it is believed to have been founded by Guru Padmasambhava: wanting to find a secluded spot for meditation, Guru Padmasambhava shot an arrow into the air and the spot where it landed was Tashiding. Tashiding has retained its tranquillity and continues to be an ideal spot for introspection and meditation. Till the Chinese takeover of Tibet, it was a place of popular pilgrimage for every Tibetan. It is the profound wish of every Buddhist in Sikkim to be cremated here. Families bury fingers, nails or even a strand of hair of the deceased in the hope that they will go to heaven.

Thikse gompa: By the 15th century, the gompas due to their riches, had become the target of invaders, bandits and non-believers. Situated strategically atop a hill in Ladakh, Thikse is a classic example of later monasteries where pragmatic considerations overruled canonical injunctions in architectural outlay.

There is a temple dedicated by His Holiness, the Dalai Lama in 1980 which has a seated image of Maitreya (the future Buddha) known in Tibetan as Chou-kor. In its background are scenes from Maitreya's life painted by the monks of Lingshed.

The main assembly hall has a room full of books and in a nearby chapel is the image of the eleven-headed Avalokitesvara, patron deity of Tibet. The gompa comes alive in winter during the annual festival. Masked dances are a must and as in all Gelukpa festivals, Dharmaraja (Dam Can-Chas Vgyal) his consort, two guardians, fierce goddesses and an array of nagas (snake gods), yakshas

♣ **LEFT:** KA NYIN SHEDRUB LING MONASTERY, BOUDHNATH NEPAL. UNDER THE DIRECTION OF THE DISTINGUISHED FAMILY LINEAGE OF HIGH LAMAS, IT HAS EVOLVED INTO A HAVEN FOR TIBETAN BUDDHIST CLERGY AS WELL AS AN OASIS FOR WAYFARERS SEEKING THE HEART OF WISDOM IN THE HIGH HIMALAYAS.

♣ **RIGHT:** TRONGSA MONASTERY, BHUTAN. THE TRONGSA MONASTERY WAS THE ANCESTRAL HOME OF THE RULING DYNASTY.

(demigods) and demons are the main characters. In the final act, a group of dancers ritually dismember the cake offering moulded in a grotesque form, signifying the destruction of evil. Thikse attracts people who come to see the gompa's oracle who speaks in Tibetan when in a trance, but can be barely comprehended otherwise.

♣ AS THE SURROUNDING DAYLIGHT FADES AWAY, PRAYER FLAGS REST IN THE TRANQUIL SPHERE OF THE SURROUNDING HILLS. TWO NUNS APPEAR IN SILHOUETTE UNDER A TREE AGAINST THE EMBER SKY IN KATHMANDU VALLEY.

♣ FACING PAGE: CARVED OUT OF THE MOUNTAINS PHUGTAL MONASTERY IN LADAKH, INDIA, IS A BREATHTAKING SIGHT. BUT HIGH IN THE SNOW CLAD ZANSKAR RANGE, IT REMAINS INACCESSIBLE FOR MOST OF THE YEAR.

Zilon gompa: This is a small gompa that is established in Dharamsala, Himachal Pradesh, which has just ten monks. What is interesting is that all the monks are ngagpa who are busy in retreat. Here one can observe tantric practices.

Thupten dorje evam Chogor: This is a monastery re-established in Shimla, Himachal Pradesh and belongs to the Nyingma tradition. Dorje drag was a famous monastery in Tibet and after the fall of Tibet in 1959, the same traditions have been continuing here under the aegis of Taglung tsetrul rinpoche. There is an emphasis on the practice of sutra and tantra here.

Rumtek gompa: Rumtek is one of the main monasteries in Sikkim and belongs to the Kagyu sect based on the famous Tsurphu monastery in Tibet. The original Tsurphu monastery was the traditional seat of the karmapas and presently, Rumtek is the biggest Kagyu centre in the whole of India, Nepal and Bhutan. Here the sutra teachings are taught through the medium of debate.

Sakya gompa: This was the principal monastery of the Sakyapas in Tibet with a long tradition dating from 1073 AD. In exile, the Sakya monastery has been re-established in Uttar Pradesh.

Drepung gompa: This was the largest monastery in the world with a population of about 7700 monks in Tibet before 1959. After exile the Drepung monastery has been re-established in Mundgod, Karnataka which is a very large Tibetan settlement today. Here the number of monks is about 3000. This is also the largest monastery of Tibetans in exile and belongs to the Gelukpa sect.

Gyumey gompa: Sherab Sengey, a disciple of Tsong Khapa in 1440 AD, founded the original monastery. The tantric tradition of Gyumey monastery was well known and has been re-established at Hunsur, Karnataka. The main topics of study are the tantric texts like the *Guhyasamaja Tantra*.